The Dun
Sixty Short Humor Stories

By John Hurst

Dedication,
To Sally Hurst Irvine

Introduction

Dunnville is a marvellous place to grow up in. To this day, quite a few of my dreams take place in that small, southern Ontario town on the Grand River: There I am, walking past the stately brick palaces along Broad Street, clad only in the childhood underwear of those innocent days. Or, there I go, sprinting down Fairview Avenue, pursued by platoons of German soldiers, fresh from television movies on a Sunday afternoon. That dream always ends in the annihilation of all Nazi wrongdoers, by my roughhouse brother, Geoffrey, or by my complicated father, Murray.

I wanted to lease a time and a place for my stories and Dunnville fit the bill. Most of my stories never occurred in Dunnville, although most of them could have. Historical figures, like Alexander the Great and Jack Benny, never lived there, but who is to say their spirits have not paid the occasional visit, say, to St. Paul's Anglican Church or to the long-vanished Victoria Hotel. Even the dead need a little adventure now and then.

The streets have often rung with martial airs, especially on Remembrance Day or on Armistice Day as it was called back when World War I was uncomfortably close in time. Luckily, no battles were fought within town limits, but the invading Fenians made it to a spot within a train ride away, in 1866. If they'd showed up, we'd have showed them!

As I have said, most of my stories never took place there. They are partly true, as far as subjects or themes can exist, but 95-percent baloney all the same.

This book could never have survived its original conception were it not for the persistent goading and pushing of my daughter, Sally Hurst Irvine. I owe all its editorial finery to Grace Darney, who must have needed all the persistence of the ages to finish that red-ink job.

(This book was edited by Grace Darney.)

To all the kind people who laughed at my stories, Wendy Welk, Deanna MacDonald and the members of the Langley Writers Guild, I owe a massive debt I can never repay; I shan't even try. To the residents of Langley Lodge, who enjoyed my monthly readings, my monthly thanks.

JH

(Because I leased creative time and space in Dunnville, I feel overwhelmingly bound to run the following story first.)

PART ONE

1. The Hiram's of Dunnville

If you drive carefully through Dunnville, down its tree-lined avenues, you will begin to notice the stately homes. Those built in the late-19th Century are planted firmly in the west end of town, far from the railroad and wartime houses in the east. All the big gothic palaces were once coveted and owned by the famous Hiram family.

Not many talk about the Hiram's these days, but beginning in 1820, before Dunnville was incorporated as an official place, Adoniram Hiram started a complicated family that dominated local history for decades.

No one knows really where Adoniram came from, but as soon as people learned his name, they realized they were dealing with an entrepreneur. As soon as his hand grasped yours in greeting, they all remember, his eyes were on you and nothing was safe – not your shillings (everyone used English currency in those days) not your farm animals, nor your comely daughters. In fact, Adoniram either knew all of these, or imagined he did. Over his long life, he managed to marry three local women and own all the livestock and livery in three counties.

The Hiram House of Refuge
One thing Adoniram knew was that in those early days, there was no safety net. One of his first business projects was the Hiram House of Refuge, which took in all kinds of unfortunates. They worked his farms for him, supplied their sons to stock the ranks of the regular army and militia, staffed all the pubs and vaudeville theatres, and married all the eligible bachelors and spinsters. Misfortune stalks us all and in those days, Mr. Hiram just waited for them to ring his doorbell. If he had too many children or servants at one time, he sold them to the First Nations. Also, he leased whole companies of young men to the Mexican army and certainly three platoons of them were at the fall of the Alamo. (They were on the winning side.) He charged higher rates for them than the Americans and sponsored whole crews of workers for the Panama Canal.

The Grand Hiram House

One of the most ornate public theatres west of Toronto, the Grand Hiram House became well known as the entertainment capital of the region. All the big names played here; Lily Langtry, Ada Isaacs Mencken, Pauline Johnson, Bing Crosby – these were the first show people to be featured in Thomas Edison's new motion pictures. The theatre's famous bar secretly dosed all beer with shots of gin and no competition ever survived for long.

The Great Fire of 1860

Reportedly started by an old woman with a grudge, this enormous bonfire made the history books because it only demolished one thing – a local goblin. The perpetrator, an Alice Emmer, set fire to Mr. Hiram and kept piling on wood until his blazing pyre lit up the skies for miles around. As soon as the victim's identity was known, local residents supplied pine trees and creosote to keep things going. Seeing the authorities arrive, Alice simply jumped in.

Happier Days, Prodigal Ways

The successor to Adoniram Hiram was his son, Almavivo Hiram, who had made his name in the wool trade. An entrepreneur like his father, he was a fair bit more experimental and had made a small fortune selling sheep wash concentrates to farmers in Europe and Asia. It is essential that your wool be clean when it's sold to middlemen and buyers, and Almavivo's concoction worked. However, it was discovered that his concentrate contained high doses of gasoline and lanolin and this combination caused many men's suits to spontaneously burst into flames, often at church.

Almavivo retired to Dunnville and to Hiram Hall, the great brick house his father, Adoniram, had built with the cheap labor from his House of Refuge. While residing in this baronial magnificence, he fell in love with the great ideal of his life, Queen Victoria. Unhappily, she refused all offers of matrimony and returned all his tokens of affection – sweaters, cashmere underwear and knobby socks – all accurately sized.

Had he simply kept to himself and taken only his own counsel, Almavivo would never have fallen into disgrace. While he made millions selling wool to Germany, he had no idea the signature on the payments of remittance would bring him grief – *Adolf Hitler*.

Modern Times

As all true revolutionaries come to know, lives lived on the edge in public usually evolve into quiet seclusion later on. Almavivo's son and successor, Almonzo, firmly set his career course into the world of finance and politics. Over the years, he quietly sponsored an assortment of national movements: temperance, prohibition and repeal, for instance. Lesser known were his ventures into model trains. As it turned out, the designers of actual trains, from steam to diesel, were a dull lot and when they needed updates, they simply turned to Almonzo's tiny coaches and locomotives for inspiration. It was the same with buses, subway cars and minivans. The real profits from public transportation went to Dunnville and never to the Mafia or the Republicans.

Almonzo remains alive to this day, despite his recent attempts to claim his own death and burial. It's believed he since changed his name to Hiramoto and assumed all mortgages owed in Japan. In the meantime, the authorities have decided it's time for a cull.

2. The Streaker of the Opry

It can take just one small change of routine to mess up the cosmos altogether. Fortunately, such overwhelming consequences can be amended soon enough, without too much scarring of the firmament.

For example, Billy B. almost messed up the cosmos years ago when he made a big mistake in his breakfast routine. Every other morning, he would pour low-fat milk into his waiting bowl of shredded wheat spoon-size morsels, with berries, cinnamon and shaved almonds. Alternate mornings, he would pour water into his waiting bowl of oatmeal, berries and cinnamon and place it in the microwave for three minutes. But, on one morning, he poured water into the shreddies and nuked them for three minutes. The result was a beige-colored mush that tasted like a cheap soufflé.

That got him thinking. What if he wore a pair of gaily patterned Speedos, rather than his formidably stern grey boxer shorts; and what if he let his wife sleep in; and what if he streaked across the back yard. That was enough. He did all three the next morning and nothing happened. His wife didn't care, it was too dark for the neighbors to notice and the Speedos twisted when he made the third lap around his property.

Three minutes in the confessional next day sorted Billy out. He never departed from his breakfast cereal routine again, but the priest kept looking at him with greater pity than usual. Eventually, Billy confided in an acquaintance, Norval S., a bachelor who pondered the matter, fiddled with his cereals as well, but then decided to take things to the next level.

During a break in a men's hockey tournament, Norval donned a full head mask, like wrestlers do, and skated nude from one end of the ice rink to the other, and back again. He disappeared for a season or two, but returned eight months later and did the ice streaking again. The second time, he did a triple lutz manoeuvre – spinning in the air and landing on the ice with a 'splat' sound – and broke his wrist. Again, he managed to get off the ice and disappear.

By the time his wrist was healed, Norval planned a triumphant return. Sneaking in to the rink, he noticed the ice had been covered with flooring for a performance by the Grand Ol' Opry. A big stage had been erected at his end of the rink, so he waited until a men's triple trio ensemble began singing, "Mockingbird Hill" and he loped across the stage, left to right.

The resulting silence was stunning. As Norval caught his breath and turned around for another run, he was amazed to see an entire platoon of policemen and volunteer firemen in hats run toward him, mostly naked and without masks. Two were female. Everyone knew them. Norval could do nothing but run back across the stage with the copy cats. They were rounded up by local media and the mayor personally shook hands with all of them, for doing the prank as a fund raising gesture for local orphans.

Norval was crushed. Everyone got recognition for the stunt on the stage, but no one knew who he was, because of his mask. In later years, he attempted streaking across the stage – at the Opry, a Billy Graham crusade and a military band concert - a few more times, but no one paid him the least bit of attention.

Finally, a group of his friends and relatives paid him a visit. The town council had been given a government grant to erect a big statue that was a cultural summing-up of the municipality. The subject could be anything, from aboriginal leaders to large watch dogs, but they were short of ideas. Norval's name came up and a bright young kid at the high school had sent in a sketch. One thing led to another and in six months, Norval had been immortalized in granite and bronze, in Rotary Park near Perimeter Street downtown. There was a dedication ceremony and he got his own photo in the local papers.

Norval got several marriage proposals after that and he finally said "yes" to Mona W., the best looking senior lady in town. They married, settled down, and he ate scrambled eggs and toast for breakfast for the rest of his life.

3. The Music of the Night

Sleep is the sweet nurse of the soul, bringing soft lullabies to the senses. Unfortunately, the sleepers are not that sweet.

If we were able to sit for two hours at the bedsides of our best friends, we would be shocked to discover that bedtime ushers in a wholly dramatic performance, with sound and fury, much like a choir backed by a full orchestra.

What follows here is a fair report of what the casual concert-goer can pick up on any given night.

Woodwinds

The Piccolo – this trilling sound is produced when the lungs produce a wheezing tonal scale, something like the approach of the angel of death. With experience, a sleeper can render it in three or four-part harmony.

The Saxophone – deep and sonorous, this arrangement can resemble many things, like a John Deere tractor in reverse, digging into a tree stump, or Cadillac transmission throwing its lugs. Some doctors think this condition, snoring, can hasten heart attacks or punches from a spouse.

The Clarinet – another highly pitched sound, this one resembles an apprentice banshee out for her first night of frightening livestock on Irish farms. It requires deep sourcing in the diaphragm.

The Harmonica – this happens when a sleeper cannot get to sleep and has resorted to cheap methods of pleasing himself. Reading silently is much better.

Brass

The Trumpet – a steady growth in maturity results in this braying sound, like a contralto singing the national anthem at a country plowing match.

The Trombone – similar to the trumpet, but the pitch and octave change when the sleeper swallows in the middle of his exhale.

The Tuba – a progression of steady grunts, no doubt inherited from ones' gorilla forbears.

Percussion

The Snare Drum – this comes into play during deeper sleep, when the sleeper makes razzberry sounds against his upper partial.

The Bass Drum – a loud eruption from the bottom exhaust.

The Xylophone – a sleeping partner's reaction to the drum, played on the head.

The Bells – resembling lunchtime at a fire house, these occur when the alarm clock goes off.

The Strings

The Violin – a rare but highly valued rush of modulated air from the nose, pronounced with the upper-class 'hnurr' accent.

The Choir

Performance Poetry – dramatic lines spoken in one's sleep, with no rhyme or beat. Commonly heard when a sleeping bride on her wedding night recites the list of her past boyfriends. The name of Genghis Khan comes up often.

The Gettysburg Address – words recited under duress by the residents of Pennsylvania.

Damnatio ab Inferno – a steady line of curses once recited by a sleeping pizza maestro.

Ghostly Moans – these occur when the spirits of old creditors enter the bed chamber.

Mumbled Suggestions – common in the sleep of defrocked evangelists.

Reciting Street Directions – these can prove upsetting, especially if they are uttered by your bus driver who is having bad dreams at the wheel.

Dream Signals

The bed sheets are tossed into the air – a businessman is dreaming his financials are being discussed in a football team's locker room.

The sleeper sits upright and says gibberish – he is dreaming of the perfect answer to the taxman.

The sleeper stands up and flies around the bed, doing the dog paddle – Peter Pan has returned.

4. No Frills: the Future of Fringe Benefits

Fringe benefits are here to stay. Their value to businesses and people is undiminished. Unions have fought and died for them. Men and women have cut their salaries to get them. To society, they are as sacred as truth, liberty or litigation. Even so…

As economies across Europe are sliding into the Atlantic Ocean, their counterparts in the Americas are tending to shore up theirs. A tidal wave of layoffs and pension cuts is expected to arrive on the eastern seaboard and crest at Mt. Rushmore.

Get ready for a new wave of dullards. This means that as surely as genetic scientists have cloned human beings to replace the boomers and everyone else, an infusion of conservative business practices is being readied to accommodate the newbies' decreased expectations.

For Americans, Canadians and Mexicans who are still shrugging off the bad effects of the 2008 Recession, the future promises a horizon as bright as Moscow in the 1950s.

Here are some highlights of "improvements" to the fringe benefit way of things.

Lump-Sum Dental Coverage
Dental employees were laid off in droves in the last recession, as millions of corporate apparatchiks lost their dental insurance when they were laid off. Now, wisely crafted fine print in the newest fringe benefit legalese stipulates that all dental coverage will amount to a lump – sum benefit that will remove all failing and crumbling teeth and replace them with permanent

dentures. So employees will be forced to either brush and floss twice daily, or baptize their new teeth nightly in Polident.

Maternity Scholarships
A valued linchpin in most women's employment rights has been that of maternity leave – often 10 months with full pay. In the near future, key activists in the women's movement will persuade millions of their sisters to use their altruistic feelings to apply for maternity scholarships. They will take maternity leave for free and forever, so that younger women will get a year's worth of experience at their jobs and on their nickel, until retirement or layoff, whichever comes in handy.

Tough-Love Family Plans
Millions of families enjoy assistance programs which get their addicted husbands, wives or children into psychology counselling and expensive rehab, which often don't work. In the new world, an ascetic tenure in the armed forces will be applied to these beloved losers. Once discharged, they will be free to marry brides from developing nations and relocate to Peru.

The Labor Day Festival
Employees of all kinds enjoy three-day weekends year round, so that they can observe holidays – ranging from Queen Victoria's birthday, to Christmas. Soon, all of these holidays will be removed, and replaced with one long weekend celebrating Labor.

Religious Apparel
There has been a lot of fuss lately over employees wearing outrageously large religious headgear and jewellery on the job. Those will be replaced with large grey dog tags bearing their names, occupations and religious affiliations.

The Family Pension Plan
Soon, retirees will be sent to live with their nearest relatives or children. That's it. The kids pay.

Homeland Vacations
Employees wishing vacations will be offered the opportunity to live permanently in their land of origin.

Hospitalization/Death Benefit
If you get sick or die, be sure to let your employer know ahead of time, so that you qualify.

Corporal Punishment
This will be granted upon request.

New Vending Machines
All snacks and candies, etc., will be wrapped in copies of the new benefit plans

5. The Case for Naturopathic Nurses

For years, the status of the naturopathic nurse has been somewhere below that of hall monitor in a Bible college, but now that naturopathic medicine has achieved full recognition, the aspiring nurselets of America are dusting off their dreams of career along with their suitcases. All are waiting for the first n-path nursing school to open.

What little girl hasn't dreamed of becoming a nurse. And what little boy hasn't dreamed of exacting revenge on one. Still, hurdles remain. There are no national standards that must be adhered to. No one knows if n-path nurses will be allowed to assist at Egyptian-style trepanning, or at First Nations bowel purges. And there remain the weightier issues – drug administration, acoustic guitars and best choice of uniforms. Should males be admitted to the sacred campus residences? What about sorority hazing by midwives?

Clearly, someone with impeccable credentials is needed to enable this unprecedented change to Western medicine. But until that happens, nursing will remain the domain of R.N.'s – registered nurses.

Meanwhile, here are some tips to help you pass the time.

Keep a watch on the politics of the times
History is full of men and women who anticipated being needed to heal the sick. They concocted medicines now lost to us and never wrote down their therapeutic procedures. They accomplished many things, removing arrows from grateful soldiers to normalizing the mentally ill. However, in times of national anxiety, these interesting souls were the first to be burned at the stake. Witchcraft is another name for naturopath-er.

Go ahead and use up your potions
It may be a long time until you can hang out a shingle. It's better to use your stores of borage now and snort as many vitamins as you can safely handle. Carry a cold compress of swamp herbs in the bottom of your purse, against the next time you can apply it to some stranger's throbbing boil. Feed some piranha oil to your worst enemy's cat. Plants treated with Piranha have more

flowers and fruit, and produce bigger harvests, especially when Piranha is used with its companion product, Voodoo Juice.

Be observant of animals
It always helps if you know how to interpret the flights of birds. For example, if crows congregate outside your home, it means you are in line for a move of residence. A pigeon that slumbers on your window sill means that peace will come to a marriage through divorce.

Get a day job
There's nothing better for passing the time than paid service to another. While all the Zamboni runs are taken, there's a growing need for the Zombie Nurse. Previously seen only at gay pride parades, these professionals have been gathering as much admiration as they had for their coming-out parties and chicken sacrifices. Modern hospital administrators hire them simply to walk around the halls; security costs have plummeted.

Observe the changing health needs of women
As women gain more job freedom in today's enlightened society, they have begun smoking cigars and pipes at an increased rate. It's not difficult to see administering testosterone to a bearded woman, or renting space to smokers' circles in abandoned warehouses.

Look for related occupations
As it may be some time before the first class of naturopathic nurses begins working in our culture, other occupations may happen sooner – naturopathic anesthetics, for example. Alternative ways of removing pain have always been rumored, such as applying Strepsils to aching teeth. Other occupations coming along are plant taxidermy, yodel therapy and communal leather chewing. Companion jobs can also be found in crime, like smuggling soy burger meat into Bosnia. The In Your Dreams Foundation routinely issues false tax receipts for prostitution, to senators of all nations.

6. The Big Threat to Female CEOs. Part One.

.

Far and away, the single most toxic threat to female chief executive officers and all women of exalted rank is the cosmic universe meltdown, in which all that exists is melted down into one, single nub of polymer.

In contrast, the biggest threat to male CEOs and all suited poohbas is a cognitive world reduced to a knowledge system based on acrylic fluff.

Both are coming, so the best tactic is to continue operations in the expanding mess that now best describes them. Lay everyone off every six months and trust in your organization.

7. Bedtime Tales for Managers

No matter how tough the life of a manager is, it's hairier still if you don't get your sleep. To counter the ill effects of sleep loss, here is a brief offering of bedtime story outlines that you can adapt to fit your own needs. While each tale bears the name of the hero, you can feel free to insert your own – unless you fear identity theft by known fairies.

Jack and the Beanstick

Tired of being paid in 'magic beans' instead of money, Jack leaves his terrible mother and sets off on a country excursion. On the very first day, he encounters a little old man who sells him a magic beanstick for some magic beans. Whatever he touches with the beanstick turns into gold.

The first thing he does is return home and whack his mother three times, neutralizing her and using the proceeds to pay off the mortgage. The next day, he plays dice with three cave trolls and touches all three with the beanstick. He takes their money as well as the extra gold and spends it in riotous living. After that, he disappears and lives his remaining days financing crusades. Losing all his fortune in an Al Qaeda swindle, he falls on his own beanstick and is repossessed by the little old man.

Jack the Client Killer

Defrauded of his real estate holdings and cuckolded by his wife's pool boy, Jack starts a new company that quickly amasses a fortune. He is created Duke of Frisbee by the king and quickly has his wife and the pool boy imprisoned. Years pass and his business grows, and Jack at length is besieged by people wanting to be his clients.

One day, an advertising wizard makes a deal with Jack. Come up with a new poem or the wizard will kill him. At his wits' end, Jack writes the following jingle:

Fee Fi Fo Booger/ Clap your hands in icing sugar/ Lick your face and you're a cougar.

The wizard rejects the jingle and makes so much fun of him, Jack pushes him under a rug, calls the police and has him put down.

Osama and the Magic Sword

Young Osama, a three-year-old warrior of Idaho, sees the Crusaders coming, to take back their lands from the people. Along with his downstairs tenant Fatima the Brave, he faces the oppressors and fights so hard they return to their homes in China. Osama later marries Fatima and they become the ancestors of many good farmers. Their secret weapon is a magic sword with a secret buzzer in the blade. The buzzer goes off when it touches an infidel.

Cinderella and the Elves
After marrying her prince and reaching adulthood, Cinderella is sent by the FBI to spy on a community of elves. Posing as a business sales person, she sells the elves a truckload of Nike running shoes. But the shoes have been coated inside with glue and the elves can never remove them from their feet. While the elves sleep, Cinderella creeps into their barracks and glues the shoes to the floor. When they wake up, Cinderella forces them to reveal their plans of conquest for the country. After she leaves, government agents deport the elves to Bogey Land.

Jack the Crazy Wizard
Jack has a great sense of humor and he is a very talented wizard. He has the uncanny ability to hypnotize people into giving him anything he wants from them. No one ever knows he steals from them – their leather jackets, their gold rings, their virginities. No one actually ever caught him and since a century has passed, everyone thinks he died and took someone's fancy tomb, to sleep forever with himself.

In fact, Jack was able to get so much from so many people, he didn't die, but retired to Arizona where he lives to this day in an invisible condo. One day, a neighbor will see him through the walls, taking a shower - and call the authorities.

Best Business Practice Tip
If you are a laid-off telemarketer, you could make a lot of magic coins by calling businesses and promising to read them bedtime stories like this, for a financial reward.

8. A Promising Telemarketing Script

.Good evening, Mrs. Pomeroy, and I hope this isn't a bad time. This is Jack Straw and I'm with Aura Optimization, a new company that takes opportunities and spins them into gold.

Do you have a minute to talk?

Yes, you do? Thanks. I'll only be a minute/ No, you have to get your nose hairs plucked? I'll only be a minute.

We are currently rewarding good people like you to post handwritten signs on your lawn that say, "Bank with Bong Kong Bank, the Wise Cracking Money Store." And quietly, later, we would give you a free repossessed SUV for your willingness and loyalty.

That's right! Just take a board or a piece of stiff cardboard, attach it to a two by four and stick it in your lawn. Then in two weeks, you can take it down and we'll be sending you your well-earned reward. Okay.

And then, if any of your neighbors want to do the same thing, just tell them to call any of our branch offices and we'll make the same promise to them.

Thanks Mrs. Pomeroy and may the Outsource be with you.

Why This Works

A grand marketing concept is at work here. People who are in the market to shop are more likely to believe what their relatives, friends and neighbors tell them, than the messages carried in the commercials on broadcast media.

For many years, most businesses have relied on newspapers first, then radio and television to churn out incitements to buy, in the form of advertising. However, in the passage of real time, too much reality has inflicted itself on consumers, leading them to suspect that the media are purveyors of fibs.

Men, women and teenagers were promised the life of their dreams – great clothes, thin athletic bodies and all the recreational sex they can handle – if they only would buy the products they advertise. The whole moneyed world bought into this and slowly, that world is getting the punch line. Consuming things sucks air into your windbag.

Now, more men and women believe their friends before they ever knowingly trust a commercial.

Even better, friends who drink coffee together also rely on good, narrative exchanges – conversation filled with great anecdotes and surprising jokes.

Opportunities for Development

Those wishing to hitch a ride on this mercantile train need only to look about them. Unless they are living in a Buddhist stupa, alone and unworried, they will belong to at least one social group. It could be a church, a bowling team or an operatic flash mob. All they need to do is spread the word about a product or service and, bingo, the whole mall is your oyster and your wallet.

People who do best at this strategy love to share stories with their friends. They are motivated from forces within them, not the promise of money and they like to try out ideas that are new.

Even better, studies have shown that selling in this way can be done without using an intent blog or website. You don't need a platform. You just need friends who will sit down with you over wine, coffee or shared interests.

Good Sales Preparation

First, always remember to smile; it often makes friends feel better. Second, always offer a free gift, like a helpful breath mint or unused tooth pick. Drop names, like Chickamauga, or Abraham Lincoln. Approach your friends like a helper, not a salesman. Try to find what their needs and problems are and dovetail your product with those. Never swear or tell dirty jokes.

Avoid closing until you have talked with them at least seven times.

Forget everything else.

9. And How Are You Today?

Most people love to explain at parties how they shut down a telemarketer. Their own pitch on the subject always gathers intensity as it surges forward, in hopes of rapt attention, acceptance and approval. And it often works: the story is told of how the hero stunned the unwary cold caller into cowed silence with an apt, pointed rebuke; storyteller and audience end it all with a smug grunt and a brief chin dip; and they go to their beds that night in gleeful, proud bravery.

It is painful to announce that the stunned silence on the phone was from disgust, not shame. The truth is the telemarketer has heard the same rebuke before, the day before that and so on. This is nothing new to the professional caller. If disturbed at all, the telemarketer is smirking at the self-delusion of his prospect, that the sky is shortly to fall on his unlovely head.

People dislike the idea of telemarketers because it represents an intrusion. In his own home and in his own head, the customer sees himself as the wisest sage who ever was, the sum of all his sums.

Telemarketers know another truth. In a day's work of making 100 telephone calls, more than 50 per cent will end up in voicemail; 20 more will get no answer at all; 15 will be politely refused; five will be rudely refused; five will meet with truly loopy people; and the last five will result in sales. Like it or not, the last segment is the best you'll ever encounter in the sales business. (Always check to make sure this adds up to make 100.)

That five percent ending in sales will wipe away all tears for the caller and make the customers forget their telemarketer party speeches.

To make this controversial sleep-stealing subject more palatable, here follow some insights calculated to benefit the perennially enraged.

And how are you today?

This question was not designed to set your teeth on edge. Actually, it was written in an innocent manner so that the sales message would be met with benign kindness. But when you hear this question, you must realize that the caller 1. Is merely reading an ancient script, much like a religious beggar who is blessing his quarry 2. Could care less how you are feeling and 3. Likely resides in the suburbs of Bombay. With wisdom and kindness, you may slam the headset down forcefully on its receiver.

Do You Have a Moment to Talk?

Skilfully posed, this question will set you into one of two camps. If you answer, "Yes, but please keep it brief," you are like most people – intelligent, perceptive and willing to have a go. But, if you answer, "No, I have to get my nose hairs plucked," you have immediately disqualified yourself from any further consideration, effort or benediction. You are consigned to the hell of all unbelievers. You will never gain the blessings of this product or service.

Shove The Phone Up Your Arse

If you use this rejoinder as a tactic, you reveal yourself as a coarse individual who never would be allowed to date or even blow raspberries on the caller's daughter. You are also in error, as a telephone once inserted into the anus of another is a sign of endearment in some countries, that welcomes the attentions of deviants and other civil servants.

Shove The Phone Up Your Arse

If a customer says this to you and you are, in effect, the telemarketer in question, simply reply, 'The same to you, sir, and with heightened momentum!" Or, "No thanks. I have already received my daily salutation and ablution." Or, "Thank you, sir. While anatomically impossible, your interesting suggestion will remind me of you always and I will take care to visit your outhouse soon."

You're Fired

This means you have inadvertently interrupted your employer in the course of her domestic duties. On leaving her premises, simply make sure you take a laptop with you until you are paid.

You Inadvertently Have Contacted a Former Spouse

Lean closely into the telephone handset, and loudly blow a bosun's whistle. It has nothing whatsoever to do with the course of business at hand, but relieves years of tension and regret.

10.   Showing Respect at Work

It's hard to believe, but today's workplace simply does not resemble the offices and factories of even 50 years ago. While laboring in the heavily wooden offices of the 1940s and 1950s was surely no picnic, there was an honest desire on the part of employees and their bosses alike to make things better.

Unions helped and so did the social workers. For decades, most of the Western world has been largely free of major world wars and technology has made the actual labor itself easier and easier.

Still, some major benefits eroded and then disappeared.

The first was respect for one's seniors. While this hearkened back to the old days when the lower classes bowed and tugged their forelocks in the presence of superiors, it persisted for centuries because it gave everyone a certain grounding in who was what and what was who. Everyone likes to work as part of a team, but teams without leaders (even better, leaders without respect) didn't last long. Employees lapsed into groups of functionaries in a work flow that never changed. All of them were surprised when, after many years of service, they were laid off while their kids were in college.

Managers, disheartened by a general lack of respect and even a minimal interest in their opinions and philosophies, shrank back into small groups of disgruntlement. Sure that they were not cherished or admired, they began to take sabbaticals and they started talking in their sleep.

The situation has been intensified by declining birth rates. Not only are employees with competence hard to recruit and retain, workers with any interest at all are invisible.

It is time that newcomers into every field let their managers know that they are valued and even worth remembering. The bosses themselves should be trying to engage their workers and reward them when they show competence.

According to Dr. Amos Phaap, a spokesman for the Sewanee Institute, "What our economy truly needs is a great depression, a famine, and an invasion from North Korea."

He says all recent studies point to a vast culture of dullness and self-absorption. Instead, what everyone needs is for all businesses to close for at least one year, and the employees to be placed, albeit humanely, in the armed forces and on farms.

"The first noticeable result," he said, "would be that in weeks, the general population would lose their weight and all stomachs would be flat. The desire of nations would be granted. But overcoming the loss of all they hold dear – their credit cards, parents, social support networks and entertainment – would take many decades."

This would require the managed growth of a culture which carries a realistic set of attitudes toward their superiors.

The newcomers of today who are working hard, raising families, paying their taxes, living independently and making sound financial decisions for themselves, should be identified, publicized and encouraged to become leaders.

"It will come," Dr. Phaap said, "not with any sinister planning, but simply by just letting things continue as they are. Everything will collapse and it will invite incursions by foreign powers."

Dr. Phaap said he and his family are just relaxing and completing courses in conversational Mandarin.

Here is a list of guidelines for surviving and even profiting from the coming social changes:

1. Take in foreign exchange students and attempt to marry them into your social support group.
2. Identify young people energetic enough to form bands of independent guerillas and get them on welfare.
3. Purge the Internet of anything that would aid and abet revolt, but never tell anyone.
4. Introduce laws repealing all codes.
5. Interest all children in agricultural work.
6. Launch homemade clothing initiatives.
7. Encourage the growing of beards without mustaches.
8. Build immense new military barracks out of existing prisons.
9. Encourage the formation and promotion of military bands.
10. Recruit fat ladies to sing patriotic songs that are adaptable to any country.

11.   Chants for the Gym and Office

Have you ever noticed that ordinary people sing and yell in public only while drunk, demented or downright stupid? You could understand that public behavior follows several simple rules – never stare, smile or talk silly – but why won't people sing? It runs contrary to their long and noble heritage.

(Admittedly, many people will yell together, but only when filled with beer at sports events. And the actual words of their cheers are real gibberish. After that, they fall asleep.)

Having to sing or yell in public reduces most people to cringing, whimpering sissies and if their ancestors could witness them, they would leave us and witness the aliens on Mars instead. Possibly the Martians are greater Irish tenors. People of today have forgotten the cheers and hymns of yesterday.

For example, during the American Civil War, 1861-1865, the ordinary Southern soldiers became famous for their Rebel Yell, a combination of high 'yips and yodelling that when used together by thousands of their comrades, drove the Union soldiers mad with fear. Yelling helped when the ammunition was low.

If you have ever served in a Scottish highland regiment, you will of course remember that when ordered, the privates would scream "A-hoigh!" before beginning a wild charge, usually downhill, at a confused enemy. They succeeded in frightening the wits out of many enemies, from the savage Iroquois confederacy to George Washington (Himself).

Standing in line with one's fellow Scots, no doubt many worried about how effeminate their voices actually sounded. But even if you had only a skinny, weasly little tenor voice, you would realize that you were surrounded by many splendid basses and baritones. The collective result was a shining example of manly ferocity. A-hoigh! Indeed.

Shouldn't the men and women of today be more proud of this ancestral talent? If they only tried it, decades of work-related depression, rejection, unemployment, low self-esteem and shyness would evaporate instantly and be replaced by a huge and surprising wave of snap, force and driving power. Anti-depression prescriptions would disappear and thousands of professional counsellors would become unemployed.

So here are a few suggestions for instilling age-old pride in our people, even the tone deaf.

A hymn for the gym
It's easy to be overwhelmed at the gym by the sheer madness playing over the loudspeakers. Ungainly men and women, hunched over, operate the exercise machines to the tempo brayed out above them. "My Sharona" and other anthems of the 1980s, rule.

If only a few of the people walked into the gym together, rehearsing the following refrain from an old Neanderthal ballad:

Stuff your Nikes, burn your Asics.
Change your tights for rags.
We're the guys from cars and condos,
We're the girls, you fags!

A chant for the carpool
Like-minded employees of enormous companies humbly show up for work each day, reminded by their bosses how lucky they are to be employed in the first place. Most of them have spent their careers, first huddled together waiting for the bus or subway; then herded in small packs from the train to a second bus; and finally hushed to cowed silence in preparation for The Boss.

If these men and women banded together into a carpool with the express intent of rousing themselves from a post-breakfast stupor, they could sing or chant the following lines:

Do you hear the people sneer?
Singing the grunts of angry toughs.
It is the point end of the spear
Who will not be fooled again!
When the going gets too rough
We will salute you with our cuffs.
That's the beginning, enough's enough
When your punishment comes!

On the way home, with growing confidence in their competence, resilience and élan, the reassured employees can chant:

Did you see how they ran
With their sweat smelling strong?
They'll all be signing up
For the next vendor with bong.

12.   Kith and Kindle

Who and what you know may never be the same. In today's exciting world of developing technology, it's getting harder to tell if the objects and people all around us are original or imitation, never mind if they're real.

To begin with, Dolly the sheep became big news in Scotland and in the scientific world at large. Experts had succeeded in bringing her to life from a clone after 277 tries. She became famous as the first domestic mammal to be reproduced without the use of sex. More likely than even that, work began on cloning human beings and so far, the results have not been made official. The reason for that were such mutations as Justin Bieber and Yahtzee the caveman. Dolly died at the age of six and they're still placing bets on Yatzee. They have elevated the Biebz long since to god status and his nibs has joined the ranks of deities, so he is now in the Downton Abbey of paradise – immune from common mortality.

Linked with that stupendous leap of human engineering came the arrival of 3-D printing. Now, using commonplace raw materials like human flesh and ear wax, entire ears and bladders have actually been printed on machines. More astounding, architects have been 'printing' entire houses, not just with composting panels in the walls that replace drains and sewers, but buildings that can be folded or unfolded and relocated at will.

It's hard to imagine, but if you don't pay your mortgage, the bank will be able to fold up your home while you are at the pub and place it back on a shelf – all over the phone. Coming home would be more than a bad dream, but a hallucination become actually real.

Fashion designers have been creating high-end clothes by just printing them. The same goes for interior décor. With a few more tweaks to the technology, you could step into a dressing machine in your own bedroom, start the correct computer program and step out again in anything from a designer suit to a Gucci bath towel.

Now comes the truly sinister part. Remember all the excitement when Oprah Winfrey began promoting the Kindle? Entire books became reduced to regimented masses of binary code so that they could be read on a computer, laptop or even on Google spectacles. Entire works of culture, from Homer's Iliad to the National Enquirer can be reduced to mathematics.

Now, put your imaginary forces to work. Take the same printing process that gave us the ear and your Aunt Minnie's elbow; reverse it with a new mechanical marvel; and reduce dear old Aunt Minnie to Kindle status.

The repercussions will take some time to digest, but so far, the benefits far outdistance the grief. Here is a snapshot view of what is sure to become a brand new revolution.

Capital punishment

Instead of taking a fearful felon to the gallows, all the authorities now have to do is call him or her on the phone, enter a binary code and suck the life keystrokes out. All the physical, emotional and mental information would be recorded on line, available to law enforcement officials and debt collectors alike. What little resulted from the physical body could be recycled into winter tires.

Modern Warfare

Instead of the stress and drain of assembling vast armies to duke it out on the battlefields of tomorrow, whole regiments of competent and capable fighting men/women could be mobilized in minutes, given the correct computer input. Fatalities and injuries could be fixed quickly, with online MASH units – pinpoint operations without the wisecracks. Following the peace talks, the armies could be stood down, cheaply and painlessly, by rekindling. And the best of all – the real civilian populations could be left alone to work, make love and conduct business while the generals and admirals play their war games.

The End to Gender War

Perennially in a state of open blitzkrieg or uneasy truce, the fight between men and women has become a secret garden of malice. The ancient art of shaming has flamed into unrestrained mobs of shameless, slogan-chanting gender fanatics, raising the hue and cry against their opposites – all outside the legal courts. It's only a few short steps to murder.

Kindling would elevate this international shame to protocol-driven dancing, in which age-old hatreds would be dissolved by the emergence of a third gender. Devoid of axes to grind and even of private parts, the third gender would come to dominate the first two and eventually supersede them. Males and females would be relegated to servant status and be artificially neutered. Kindle people would survive to rule the future.

Friends and Lovers

It is a true statement and worthy to be believed, that people cannot choose their relatives, but may select their friends. With rekindling, even the most needy individual could summon up a perfectly designed friend – for anything. A teenager could bring a dazzling lover into the home, and it is returned to a library online just before the parents get home. A little girl with the hidden shame of having only imaginary friends, or window pane friends, could do the same. Friends could be supplied by non-profit associations, or by criminal cartels. This is a cue to money seekers everywhere.

Imagination

It would die out until something better could be programmed.

13.　　The Kink in My Cord

No matter how much excellence is produced each day by the human animal and no matter how high the goals, one element always remains: human garbage. Therefore, the work, the craft and the employment of the commercial janitor will likely be around forever. As a best bet, the job market will always offer this opportunity to the energetic - and security to the walking dead.

Knowing the required skills is often paramount; night school is the best way to learn them. The first hard fact one always learns is this – never mix chlorine bleach with ammonia. It immediately produces chlorine gas which is demonstrably fatal. You inhale, all around you turns olive green and you are greeted by your coughing ancestors.

With that uppermost in mind, your first task is always this: on entering the office, turn off the alarm before you turn on the lights. Otherwise, loud sirens will greet you and sleeping employees will stalk the halls for you, carrying baseball bats.

Have Your Extension Cord Exorcized.

Now for a real bogeyman. The next big thing is this: ask your parish priest to bless your 100-foot extension cord. It's this way, see. Left unattended, an extension cord will slowly curl up on itself, using long settled kinks to create an incredible series of knots. It begins to resemble a cross between an octopus and Medusa the Gorgon. It will quietly wrap a loop around your left ankle as you vacuum an office, and then trip you into falling directly onto your beak. Then, it will pull office partitions down, one after another, and they will shatter pottery, prized photos of goggle-eyed children, half-cups of cold cafe latte, hidden ashtrays and bushels of secreted vending machine coins. While providing an honest look into the privacy of office employees (civil servants are the grubbiest) this calamity causes hours of unwanted work.

Extension cords, not ghouls or gossips, are the devil's spawn. Always remember to place your cord ahead of you in the direction you wish to vacuum, and then neatly curl it into yard-long loops when you are done.

What to Wear When High Dusting

There's an etiquette to high dusting. Always make sure you wear a hat. One never knows what will drop on your head when you dust. It could be a hidden $20 bill or a large mouse. Also, wear tops with sleeves. In the presence of office workers, a high-reaching janitor never flashes her armpit, shaven or not.

Cleaning in the Land of the Nerds

One rare treat is the chance to improve on the hygiene habits of geeks and nerds. These special people congregate in labs and virology labs and are the clean-squeakiest. In addition to being very picky, these eccentrics are also very funny. One vice president I had the privilege to meet has a sign on his office door proclaiming his title – Senior Antedeluvian.

An important tip: when cleaning for these employees, always draw maps of their desks, accurately depicting which items belong where. Otherwise, they will be misplaced and when this outrage is discovered, Earth, its firmament and the Heavens will be altered forever.

They have their own jokes, always neatly printed in black marker strokes on a white board: "Anti-microbials should never be used, because bacteria is the only culture some people have."

"A physicist, biologist and chemist all go to the beach. The physicist decides to study the currents and fluid dynamics of the waves. He goes into the water and drowns. The biologist decides to study the aquatic life of the ocean. He goes into the water and drowns. The chemist takes out his notepad and writes, "Physicists and biologists are soluble in ocean water.""

Some Personal Advice

- If you think you are too fat, get measured. A waist more than two axe handles wide requires Vaseline smeared on door frames so you can pass through.

- If you discover employees having sex, never interrupt them. Always work silently around them, using your best mime skills. Never ask them for a cigarette. Never offer assistance. Cameras should be left in your pocket.

- Never eat leftovers in the lunchroom. There are surveillance cameras galore and few things cause more violence than to be seen stealing a receptionist's breakfast.

- The best time to dust furniture is an hour before sunset. Horizontal solar rays will illuminate each and every mote of dust, as well as highlight gum on the carpet. If you need entertainment, try forceful bodily emissions when dust is hanging in the air.

- When cleaning gum from carpets, the exceptional janitor will neither leave no residue, nor sample the wad.

- While washing windows, always keep your cleanser close to you. Some lawyer or tax accountant will always try to save it for aperitifs.

- When asked to help employees in their jobs, politely refuse. This applies especially to prison guards, graffiti artists and teachers marking exam papers.

14.   Preaching Jihad in the Workplace

A new white paper from the Sewanee Foundation for Right Ordering provides increased evidence for the decline of authority across all kinds of businesses in western nations. The document, *A Case for Corporal Punishment and Indentured Servanthood*, was released on Friday and quietly distributed among corporate boards and business schools.

Case studies that clearly outline acts of employee insurgence across North America have top executives worried and their security chiefs have begun monitoring employees who preach 'disobedience jihad' against any person whose name appears on a company's flow chart.

The report says that incidents involving second guessing, micromanaging and sheer physical groping of both sexes now originate among the ranks of underlings and not from the offices of the business elite. Those managers who formerly bullied their employees are now reporting to work with security staffers and in the case of much smaller businesses, with their mothers to protect them.

"Actually, it's a polite form of air rage," said Dr. Amos Pfaap, a Sewanee spokesman. "Decades of sensitivity training for managers have enabled bullies of all sorts to emerge from the corporate matrix and take advantage of the more attentive bosses. And with the rapid decline of military-type executive administrations, the more woolly-headed managers have unknowingly lost control. And who among them would even dare to launch a human rights lawsuit from the top down, knowing the media will hoot them into unemployment."

In corporate North America these days, just about any strong-willed man or woman can terrorize a polite manager simply by waving a stuffed teddy bear in their face. And the reverse is even more chilling: cases of managers who have lost control and charged screaming at their employees while brandishing belts and suspenders; they have been mobbed, and their trousers removed. Many are never seen again.

Female executives are as vulnerable to abuse as their male counterparts. The Sewanee Foundation paper cites documented cases of women managers being held down by swarms of women, who typically fasten "paper trails', long records of their alleged sins, to their backs. These documents are typically printed on rolls of toilet paper. Other female managers have endured unwanted cosmetic and hairdo makeovers and their actual lip mustaches have been waxed off by jeering tormentors.

Sewanee says that some companies are quietly fighting back. Teams of ex Green Berets have been hired to cause dissention among the trouble makers. This is worked up by female moles who lure activists of either sex into compromising positions that can be videoed and used against them. Danger spots here are any flat surface where lusty misbehaviour actually occurs, and underneath desks. Veteran Navy Seals have been used to grope male rebels and remove their pants. Professional mercenaries who remove thongs have been recruited from Iran.

In the most common cases, involving such verbal abuse as micro managing (focusing on an employee's personal habits rather than their work) or second-guessing (repeatedly countermanding employee decisions), managers are now being coached to act tough. Private contractors are now making millions of dollars in secretly teaching corporate managers to retake control of their departments.

Some of the course descriptions are revealing:

- How to roll your eyeballs back to simulate mental patient ferocity.

- How to walk around a desk slapping brass knuckles into your chest – and mean it.

- How to remove an employee's wigs, false teeth and false boobs without leaving a mark.

- How to make false debt collection phone calls over a loudspeaker.

- Forcing trouble makers to do pushups, serve coffee and join bible studies.

- Sneering class – basic level, intermediate with a nasal twang, and senior grunting with naughty remarks

- Finding embarrassing Facebook party photos of unruly employees and making them screensavers for the entire workforce.

The white paper also gave details of local movements to restore social class boundaries to the workplace, limiting movements up or down. America for centuries has been famed for the life successes of entrepreneurs who rose from obscurity and poverty to make millions in commerce. Now, the stories of Andrew Carnegie, Thomas Edison and Justin Bieber will be relegated to mere legend.

Many companies are seeking to restore the English mannerisms of the 18th Century to the working class – rougher language and pronunciation, drab living conditions and reduced medical care, to curb bad behavior among ordinary employees. Increased military service will be introduced, with a marked officer class to lead it.

"It would be much like 'The Simpsons' for them, but in black and white," Pfaap said.

Indentured servant hood, a centuries-old system requiring common folk to undertake menial jobs for room and board instead of wages, would replace union apprenticeships. Home ownership would be abolished, with a return to slums.

"Certainly we expect some opposition," Dr. Pfaap commented, "but one has to look on the bright side – the survival of commerce itself."

15.   The Renegade Martial Arts

When you put out the garbage late at night and you think you hear faint cheering and screaming, it's not for you to worry. All is well and things are as they should be. That far-off noise is an athletic crowd cheering on some teams of renegade martial artists. They have been around for years, embittered men and women who strip to the waist and fight dirty for their peers.

Martial arts have been going on for many years, since before 2000 B.C., but they have not been noticed until quite recently because of their secretive nature. The oppressed peasants on Okinawa learned how to fight back against their feudal muggers by getting strong and sneaky. Their product – *karate*. The ancient Israelites worked up a fighting form known as *abir* and over time, their abusers learned not to mess with them. Indeed, at one point, compared with an abir champion, the lone Roman legionary was a sissy.

All forms of martial art have been developmental and since their discovery by Western culture in the 1800s, they have gone underground again. These days, obscure forms of the warrior arts have quietly flourished among the professions and trades. Low-profile tax accountants wage their own private wars with *knuckle-dime* – inserting dimes into one's fists to create lethal weapons, and Eli Wapple, the father of baristas, went without sandwiches at lunch so he could practice his own art, *macchiato* – inserting dairy products into customers' body openings without being detected.

Martial arts in the other professions are legendary and often, mere rumor.

Recently, wall paintings in the world's subways have glorified The Voover, a local word mix that combines *vacuum* and *Hoover*. This celebrates the world champion of the annual Janitorial Games, in which government heads of state place bets on fights by men and women who use stripped-down cleaning devices to murder each other on the graveyard shifts of the world. Linked to criminal elements, these games somehow get closed-circuit television coverage around the world and the finals, played last year in Singapore, saw Wun Nguyen of Hanoi defeat Murray Pye, a Scot, in a vicious duel of poisoned plungers.

Electric shocks can be applied to an opponent when the weapons of choice are carpet steamers. This works best when the opponent is prone and unconscious. Vacuum cleaners have been modified into short-range bazookas, hurling projectiles that can snip off an enemy's backside, if the aluminum tubing is replaced by brass, and steel wool is wrapped around pebble-projectiles.

The storied world of retail banking has long been a hotbed of naked aggression. Branch managers have been known to take customers by the shoulder, hustle them across the street from a competitor's office and brutalize them into taking out accounts in their own dens. Known as *orcas*, these managers in black suits and white shoes (bankers even today still haven't grasped the basics of fashion) have been compared to killer whales who play `catch` with seal pups. In private, the bankers refer to the new customers as *pucks*, to be slapped about without mercy. Their subordinates act as *aides*, tripping pedestrians and rolling them to the curb, and as *angelic rescuers*, who direct them to the team's branch office.

This toxic form of bank competition is called *accounts inconceivable*, because the organizers, all bankers, were unable to create a simpler name. However, the usage in Asian banking circles favors the more apt *pimp-ology*.

On the blue-collar side, wide open ergonomics vie with the immutable laws of gravity as the roofers of the world fight for a championship of their own. And for them, few things are more exciting than doing body slams on steep roofs.

Watch for them as they grapple each other on a roof beam, then fight to grab lighted torches to flame the losers.

In a world of closures, the drivers of a funeral hearse often are put to work on maintenance tasks, like polishing urns and trying on surplus socks after cremations. But the vehicles themselves, weighing at least 5,000 pounds and reaching maximum speeds of 100 miles per hour, are getting an anxious try-out by one of the world's most secret, black-ops outfits.

Hearse drivers first came to government notice when they were observed driving down country roads at insane speeds. Next, when some of the more tech-savvy chauffeurs figured out how to make their hearses invisible, the CIA sent in observer teams immediately and enrolled their top killers in funeral career courses. Eventually, some of their brightest people learned the ancient secrets of *corpse wagons* and began recruiting some of the veterans.

These days, government agents make up at least 30 percent of real funeral attendant teams. That's why a hearse that is blocking traffic and holding up lawful mall shoppers, often can suddenly morph into a lady pushing a baby buggy, or a little girl on a bike. (No, you're not crazy, or drunk!)

16.   You're Doing Everything Right

Counsellors need more bucking up than anyone else. At a moment's notice, they may be required to provide solace to a grieving pit bull owner whose precious pet has been poisoned by a group of grannies, and a few minutes later, to putting to rest the silent fears of a failed Mafia hit man. The range of emotions is staggering and ultimately exhausting.

No matter what counsellors may learn through years of academic training, they never will be quite ready to handle any needy person who stumbles through their office door. For example, it's often wise to simply sit back and let the patient talk, but quite another thing when the patient tires of your calmness and starts tossing your potted plants out the window. (*A classic cry for help.*)

Experience is often the best teacher, but not if you get killed or fired in the process. For example, what's good about learning not to giggle during moments of a patient's personal reflection, when you're standing in line at the food bank after being terminated for foul practice?

Perhaps the most useful tool in getting through these challenges is to keep a private tip list. For example, if you are often forced to give healing thoughts to shaking lawyers who have developed a morbid fear of passing dwarves in hallways, write, "Crouching low, weave and blow" as a handy tip for writing on their palms with a ballpoint pen. Or, "duck, duck, goose, goose".

So here is a list gathered from many years of shepherding fearful people through the dark passages of life.

Terrorists are People Too
Remember that even though Osama Bin Laden had several wives, he never had a friend. It's just that no matter how much noise they make, no matter how they get noticed by the media, terrorists are just used to beating up old ladies and kids. When they have to face trained soldiers toe to toe, they don't like life very much. That's their weak point and where you can shoehorn your talk.

The Mean Little Kid
You have to get physical. If you exhaust all your techniques, invite him to lie down on the carpet. Then sit on him for a while.

Healing for the Depressed
Sometimes patients with depression just sit there, not once responding to your advice and effervescent wit. The thing to do is change their music. Invite them to join you in a singalong, but skip the campfire songs, like "Three thousand bottles of beer on the wall". Instead, try "Does Your Chewing Gum Lose its Flavor on the Bedpost Overnight," followed by "My Wild Irish Rose".

Shock Treatment
Instead of getting your patient to endure the horrifics of Nurse Ratched in the operating room, just shuffle up to him on the carpet and touch your finger to his ear. Then teach him how to remove his own earwax with an electric nose hair clipper.

The Field Trip

Six large men in diapers walk into your office together. The thing is, wait until you have exhausted all their sharing, and then pile them into a city bus and ride the whole route. After one ride, leave them alone for another trip while you get lunch. After their third trip, send them back to their hockey practice where they began.

You're Doing Everything Right

This is a wonderful catch-all phrase, because it gives the patient the reassurance that deep down, she's fine after all. Also, it tells the poor person that no matter how bad things are, she should keep up the good work.

17.   Whassup? Supporting Our Local Police

For some very good reasons, the outward face of our police officers is as smooth as a freshly shaved Rottweiler. Policemen and women are a taciturn lot, much like the infantry soldiers of old, because they have to function quickly in return for many rude surprises. No one likes to see a cop gape in the face of sudden peril or alarm.

It's no surprise then, that members of our police forces are susceptible to heavy drinking; it is surprising that more officers don't drink, but bathe in alcoholic drinks after a full day's work – seeing us all at our worst. How could any sane human being react otherwise when returning home from a shift of herding dozens of perverts off the buses and into clean cells, or after preventing thousands of Occupy marchers from fouling our cities' commerce.

Actually, their psychological makeup is just the same as any other honest job force group. Police then would be 10 percent homosexual, 10 percent alcoholic, 30 percent female and 80 percent socially shy. The numbers don't add up because more in all ranks would not admit to occasional fibbing on questionnaires and to being anxious about arithmetic. Even worse, they have been given a bad reputation by the thousands of uniformed security guards who abuse their snack choices by eating too many doughnuts. Real cops actually eat jerky and will do that for you to prove it's true.

So here are some suggestions for how to behave around police officers in a positive and supportive manner.

1.   Never yell `Bang!` in the presence of law enforcement personnel.
2.   If you are playing next to an erupting fire hydrant, always let a policeman play too.
3.   When indulging in face painting, try to avoid heavy metal grimaces and demonic glares. These are very upsetting. Instead, apply soft pastels to your cheeks, and little rosebuds, so you look inoffensive and charming.
4.   If a police officer rings your doorbell, always open the door and ask, `Wassup.` This will convince him you have nothing to do with whatever is going on around you. (This word by the way has been in the Oxford Dictionary for two years now.)

5. Never ask a police officer for a date. Instead, ask the sergeant. He is wiser and has a higher pay grade.
6. If a bum asks you for a smoke, but has clean breath and freshly washed ears and nose, he's an undercover cop and probably his wife launders his shorts. It's your cigarette, but be careful you don't give him more. Never encourage bad habits.
7. Some cops work in Black Ops. These are operations which require stealthy sneaking around and descending on ropes. If you see this, you are in New York, or in a bad dream.
8. If you see a team of cops running in single file, chanting `Hut, hut,` they are actually practicing community relations for a visit to the local roller derby.
9. In a real emergency, never call `911!` Dial it on the phone instead.
10. Do not use bad language when speaking to the police. They will assume you're family.
11. If you see a dead body on the sidewalk, never draw around it with chalk. Real professionals use invisible ink that turns white in the presence of idiots.
12. If you want a real laugh, wrap a police car in yellow incident tape with the driver inside.
13. In the presence of witnesses, rename your dog Velcro.
14. When out strolling with your grisly chums, always show your tattoos to the cops. Everyone likes modern art, even if you did it.
15. Never moon a passing police car. The police don't need any more new jokes.
16. Always be clean. There is nothing worse than a drug-sniffing police dog checking out your suitcase, then peeing on it.
17. Never kiss a police dog named Butch.

18.   The Case for Ending Customer Loyalty Programs

The problem with all customer loyalty card members is that they are like most real people – they'd rather sit around and not do anything. The best reason for this is that it allows them to seem composed, diligent and peaceable - and not likely to get into any trouble. But the companies with loyalty programs want their customers to literally jump up and down in anticipation of new and more exciting benefits ahead. What a disconnect!

Loyalty is founded on trust for a good outcome. Most soldiers will follow their general, if they know he'll probably win. Customers of businesses will continue to shop from them, if they know they will get items they want, at low prices and with no chance of spoilage. But what do loyalty programs offer them? Trifling price reductions, an emailed newsletter, or chuckled moans of fake esteem, that's what.

In fact, most people carry loyalty cards in their wallets, from all the supermarket chains in town at least. When they flash a card to a checkout beauty queen, the customers are appealing to their first belief – you'd better gimme or I'll never love you again.

Loyalty cards are backfiring all over the free world, even though they are used in the most unsuspected places.

Cardholder Quincy Dobbs, an inmate in a private prison, was having trouble with volunteer Brother Freidhelm, of MOGO, (Mennonites of the Grim Observance) staying overnight. In fact, the good brother came with the cell. There was no escaping his malevolent gaze: no horsing around here, or Brother Freidhelm would whack you with his big black cowboy hat. He'd keep it up until you were let out on Mondays to rejoin your family. (Private prisons cater to people with intense guilt feelings, or to bad little children who say 'no' and 'shut up' to their mothers.)

Mr. Dobbs, who had a loyalty card with Reformatox, a huge international corporation, threatened his jailers that he'd switch to Jolly Jailer, a Dubai start-up, unless they replace the grim Mennonite with a Bedouin torturer of the same sex. We know Mr. Dobbs won his case, because Brother Freidhelm has launched his own anti-defamation website and book store.

Another case involved Denise Wonga. She had been elected grand wazoo of a transplanted New Zealand Maori tribe that had decided to emigrate and give life in Utah a try. She had attempted to enroll her members in the Mormon religion, but its leaders turned her down, stating they would not allow the worship of snake gods, no matter how inclusive their loyalty cards were.

Grand Wazoo Wonga appealed to the openness of a competing loyalty card firm that agreed to the snakes, but forbade the wearing of furs or the bashing of pinatas stuffed with firecrackers.

"It's the idea that counts here, not the other stuff," the loyalty firm announced, in pronouncing the sanctity of her religion.

Some entrepreneurs have made money from sub-letting customer loyalty IDs. For example, Esprit Radisson, of Bellingham, Washington (her actual nom de plume) is a paid-up member of the Ardent Matchmaking Service. She has found that charging members of her own network for the IDs and contact data of her dates more than pays twice over her annual Ardent membership. In actual fact, for every date, she will reap seven private enquiries and currently, her marriage rates are twice as high as those claimed by Ardent.

This situation, while admirably entrepreneurial, runs dead against the laws of the land which state these days that any child of a marital union must be able to trace the facts of how one's parents met, in order to legally claim monies or properties from any inheritance. Lawyers these days are more likely to be interested in how the mother met the father than in whether the claimants are merely little bastards.

While the case of Radisson vs. Ardent case will likely be on appeal for decades, most lawyers are betting on Ms. Radisson, who holds a loyalty card from Ardent. The card promises rebates on all dinner bills that did not result in marital intercourse. In the end, she either gets the rebates – or the alimony from several thousand bridegrooms.

19.   How to Conduct a Proper Interview

Some magazine interviews are failures from the start.

The subject of the interview answers your questions with plastic, press-release statements and they are so plausible and tranquillizing, you might have to be awakened before the end.

All readers of your report deserve a better deal, even if the interview subject is asleep too.

Here is a list of sure-fire suggestions that will keep the interviewee awake and at the same time, convince the readers they should buy the magazine's next issue.

1.   Always be considerate of your subject

Many interviewers are too fond of their subjects. You must resist the temptation to pat down his or her lapel, or to smooth down an errant lock of chest hair. Always remember to allow an imaginary 12 inches between yourself and the person who has bravely stared down 12 internal demons before agreeing to submit to your interrogation. It's much like getting along with other passengers on a dangerously overcrowded Asian ferry. One misstep and you could have an awakened madwoman speaking fluent Baboon, gnawing at whatever appendage of yours looks like lunch. Nervous ticks and blinks are a sure tipoff that this is a walking volcano that could be set off.

2.   Prepare yourself for an excellent experience

A useful method of preparation is working up to a serious attitude toward the interviewee and his area of expertise. At first, try to pretend that the person actually matters. It may take a little while, but eventually you will reach a state in which you can take this person seriously. Imagine him or her as the senior bastard in your workplace: one mistake, one unforeseen giggle and you'd go from sitting primly in a chair while wearing a suit, to pushing a shopping cart in the street and picking up aluminum cans.

3.   Select a reliable recording device

Never go into an interview taking down notes, unless you are an adept shorthand wizard. Always use an analog tape recorder and play it back later when you are writing your report. Notes in your own handwriting are accurate only .06 percent of the time; the remainder depend on your moods during the interview, shifting with the daydreams in your mind, or the subject's. There are two worst outcomes: you doze off during the subject's answer and he has to shake your shoulder; your gaze becomes fixed on the subject's cleavage, male or female, and the subject has to snap his/her fingers in an upward motion, to shake off your dream mode and focus on the face. Not funny and absolutely true. Decide at the outset of the interview if your subject has a fascinating chest and is worth the trouble.

4.   Carry a list of emergency questions

In case your interview subject goes off on a technical tangent during an answer, always be prepared to announce the following: "Says you!" While impertinent, it clears the decks for immediate clarification and it wakes you up.

5. Be prepared for emergencies

Many unfortunate events can occur, even when your subject is intensely interesting and you are actually focused for a change. There could be a fire drill. Earwigs could fly up your subject's nose. He/she could suddenly grip your knee and turn out the lights. (The best antidote here is an air horn.) Always keep your hands holding something; that prevents your thumbs from twiddling. But in the end, always remember one thing – your subject is more scared of you than you of him/her.

6. Never interview any animal.

At least, never get caught interviewing an animal. The worst are birds that get drunk from eating fermented blueberries and have crashed into your office window. At best, their comments are confusing and always off topic.

7. How to find out if your subject is terrified

Check out his fingers. If they are shaking, check yours first. There may be an earth tremor in progress, or his office printer may be grinding its plastic splines. Or your quivering fingers may betray a deep-seated terror in your own heart. If his face is pallid and sweating, you may have broken wind. Or he may feel one coming on himself. If his/her eyeballs roll back, lean back in your chair and call for the company nurse. If you pass out in the process, the health problem is yours. Always be alert for the telltale smell of gunpowder; it's either a terrorist bomb or he's got lunchtime yogurt on his breath. If he starts singing a nursery song in the middle of his answer, he's retrograded to an unpleasant childhood and may lunge at you. Get him in a headlock and drag him out to the receptionist's desk.

8. Always leave the receptionist a card.

In a pinch, the nine of clubs always works. It's the most pleasant one and has the best graphic items.

9. Kiss your job goodbye

20.   Media Relations 101

When you consider the role of public relations, in your business or in your life, you must agree that if there were no problems there would be no need for public relations (PR). And contrary to popular thought, PR is not done with smoke and mirrors – or even mirrors.

There is a second part to these over-arching thoughts: public relations workers are the most susceptible to dementia of all in the work force who dress like them. It's like all men wearing kilts will eat oatmeal at some point in their day.

The most stressful part of PR is media relations. Keeping in touch with the media is like keeping the faith with your company and with all the buzzards in the surrounding trees. When speaking to the media, you must speak with one voice, respond to questions as quickly and as smoothly as a drugged lizard and you must have access to counselling at all times.

The golden rule is this. Never Screw Up on a Slow News Day.

Here are some case studies to underline the rules. The first result must always be assumed – plan vs. results - results always trump plan.

The Heavens are Sounding
In the 1990s, a major corporation decided to rely on computer-driven technology to issue news releases on a staggered time basis. The contents of the release depended on which markets around the globe were contacted first. So stories were configured for automatic release every 59 minutes – midnight for London and noon for Shanghai, for example.

For reasons only known to the spirits, a huge solar flare suddenly occurred, causing the computer technology to issue all news releases at the same time – midnight. The contents of each news releases were received gladly around the world, but the tech team behind the software was sacked.

Look to Your People
A major news announcement was forthcoming from a huge international company and it was focused on the simultaneous release of information to local news media serving areas surrounding the company's industrial plants. Having learned from the solar flare incident, media relations gurus decided to trust written statements on paper, delivered by actual human beings.

As it turned out, all deliveries were refused about the same time. Each information package was delivered C.O.D. – cash on delivery. It had to be re-sent by a backup email system. Result - the entire mailroom management cadre was fired.

Double-Truck Destruction
A city's premier haberdasher wanted more business share, so it decided to buy advertising in the local newspaper. It paid thousands of dollars for two full-pages of ties, suspenders, socks and shirts. Two huge words were used in the purple headline that ran across the top of each page. The type size had not been used since war was declared in 1941. SHIRT SALE.

They left the 'R' out of shirt. Next day, the entire haberdashery was sold out. The printers were sacked. A union was voted in and forever after, the merchants got to check the ads first.

Check the Headlines
A news release for a huge corporation was being kept secret, in case something went wrong and it had to be issued to the media. Things did, as they usually do, go wrong and the release was mailed to all news media at the same time. Its headline stated explicitly – Not For Release to the Media.

All the media ran the release. They weren't about to be fooled, so the company was forced to fire an executive to make the headline come true.

Wholly Unholy
One of the more famous rules of the 10 Commandments is the seventh – Thou shalt not commit adultery. In the 1600s, one of the first editions of the King James Bible was issued. It read: "Thou shalt commit adultery.'

King James was not amused and several printers were hanged.

21. How Dentists Made it Through the Recession

The office floors of North America are littered with the debris of professional tragedies from the 2008 Recession. Unfinished café lattes in the landscaped offices. Toilet paper rolls in the office lavatories, dust covered and frozen in mid yank. Fashion magazines with models now hopelessly out of style. Laid-off professionals still singing dirges in choirs somewhere.

But no archaeological find from those dark days can equal the items left behind in the office suites of dentists. Stacks of elderly newspapers. The employment records of laid-off receptionists and dental hygienists. Buckets of repossessed dentures. And the saddest of all – a solitary dentist with less than 10 patients. They all point to an unemployed workforce stripped of its dental insurance policies when the corporations failed.

Maybe there are sadder sights than a dentist making his own upper plates and having to wear them with the teeth inserted backwards, but these are few.

Happily, many dentists emerged from the Recession with their grit and pluck intact. Like the pioneers of old, they simply blazed new trails. Some converted their offices into travel agencies for recent immigrants from Bosnia, aching to return to the comforts of home. Others became telemarketers for emigration lawyers, seeking malcontents to banish to Bosnia.

Here is a brief survey of success stories from the legions of unemployed dentists.

The Travelling Flosser

Can you imagine a personal tooth flosser to the stars? No one ever could before. Dr. Ibrahim VanBlint, a Belgian, actually took a Hollywood star mansion tour, and then walked the whole route the next day with a briefcase full of dental floss. Doorknocking for days, he was able to conduct free demos on the likes of Renee Zellweger, Kim Basinger, Lassie and the mummified corpse of Joe E. Brown. Today, he personally supervises squads of laid-off dentists as they floss thousands of famous mouths, and he now drives to his appointments. Dr. VanBlint is opening franchises in Palm Springs and Vancouver. After that, who knows? Maybe he'll sign up rich people who are not famous.

Downmarketing precious metals

What about all those fabled stockpiles of unused gold and silver; those deep urns of expensive composite ceramics? They once were destined to fill the dental cavities of millions, but now? Try looking for them on the iPods and eyeglasses of the rich. Three dentists, the Mendicant Brothers – Marcus, Brutus and Doug – developed a method of fusing the fillings to portable phones and other personal necessities, in the same way mother-of-pearl was added to the handles of repeating revolver pistols. There's a lucrative repeat business here, in that the fillings, just like crowns, tend to fall off in 8-10 years.

Bringing Smiles to the Fallen

Ever wonder what happened to the pain killers? There's a quiet but huge resale market to the thousands of psychologists who used to despair over the worsening symptoms of their patients. First, nothing beats the blues like novocaine. The dentists apply it to wild-eyed sufferers and then place them in a pleasant but padded room for eight hours. Imagine having no pain, no matter how hard one bangs his head against walls and kitchen cabinets. And when you are troubled, how about inhaling nitrous oxide – laughing gas. Dr. Aaron Smelp, the originator of this concept, had a big problem relieving the dentists themselves of this furtively used medicine. It had become their last defence against depression and sinus overload.

Actuarial Betting Parlors

Remember how wealthy Romans used to pay to watch gladiators kill each other with big boo-boo knives? Well, taking a cue from those ancient deviates, Dr. F.X. Porfirio came up with a more sophisticated sport. Generate huge sums of money by encouraging teams of ordinary citizens to place money bets on individual dentists. The idea is to wager how long each dentist would live as an ordinary citizen. For the most part, they simply observe as those poor unfortunates grind out their lives toward the commonplace end – heart attacks, obscure geriatric homes or unstamped passports.

Leasing the kids

This is effective in those troubled teen years.

Open a for-profit prison

Cleaner and safer than Corrections Canada, profitable prisons run by dentists are pure money factories because they accept innocent people on weekends.

22.   Some Tips for a Male Underwear Model

Every young man is a male underwear model in his own eyes. In fact, there are posers in front of the bedroom mirrors of the nation that would put even Vladimir Putin to shame. (Even he had to start somewhere.)

But few of these aspiring underwear models have ever made it to the Sears catalogue and glory. Most have dropped out along the way, for a variety of shocking reasons.

Expert Dr. Isadore Schlotkin says some of them can't bear to stand close to comely female models in their bras and briefs for those popular 'duet' poses. Others are too ashamed of their birthmarks, acne scars, tiny genitals and ingrown body hairs to give the profession a try. Even more are too afraid to strip even past their hats and scarves for fear of ridicule.

"It takes guts to peel off your jeans and socks in a big photo studio," says Dr. Schlotkin. "Inwardly, your soul is shrieking 'Judge me! Judge me!' to that crowd of women standing there with their arms folded in amazement."

Don't Fight Genetics

It's much better to begin when you are three years younger. Right after puberty, you will get a rather good idea of how you will look. Sorry, but you must have well-proportioned limbs and an athletic build. If pot bellies and spaghetti legs run in your family and every male in your family tree is bald, it's better to go into dentistry or law.

Trust Routines, Not the Internet

Consign yourself for the next three years to (1) a good gym and (2) a spa that will accept men. Have your hair styled and your skin worked up. Combine a sensible regimen of weight training and aerobics, but don't go crazy over it. (It's better to have the shape of a soccer player than that of King Kong.) Have your teeth fixed, capped, or whatever you need. Use a dentist and stay away from those internet surgery rip-offs. Never try to fix your teeth yourself. Read all the men's fashion magazines and learn how to be cool. Get a steady day job.

Off With the Pants

Before you sign up for an expensive photo shoot and prepare a portfolio of yourself, scan the news outlets for non-profit organizations that publish nude calendars to raise funds for themselves. Usually, the models are loopy ladies with 1890s hair styles and the men are pitiably endowed specimens. Join these groups and try to get picked to pose nude the following calendar year. This doesn't cost anything and you'll make lots of lifelong friends along the way, as you save the spotted whales or help get rich kids out of Mexican prisons.

Circulate the calendars with a nude photo of you. Send them not only to the retailers of men's underwear, but to the manufacturers as well. This may get you modelling work a year before you need to pay for a photo portfolio. Bon chance! Do more calendars.

Here are a few tips to smooth your way.

1. At the spa, invest in depilatories for your body hair. If you come from a region anywhere southeast of France, get waxed all over, all the time, front and back.
2. If your eyebrows run together above your nose, divide them in the middle.
3. Your penis should be as long as your thumb; if longer, charge more.
4. To look cool, always try for a facial expression that suggests you are sniffing cabbage.
5. Remember to care for your feet and toes. No toenail painting, no matter your friends.
6. Watch the nose hairs. Kill 'em.
7. Lose the aftershaves and eaux de colognes.
8. Eat nothing bigger than your head.
9. Learn all you can about the industry and its background characters. Avoid the crooks.

23.   Signals from the Sales Floor

It's hard enough for a human being who has been vacuumed up from private life to work in the vast retail trade, but harder still to become fluent in the specialized art of discreet signalling on the sales floor. It's even harder than that for new employees to remain complacent when all employees around them are engaged in physical motioning and whistling in a tightly competitive space.

To begin with, retail businesses with enormous sales floors must create communications among employees and their supervisors that do not distract or confuse their valued customers. For example, word of a huge dollar discount could result in a crowd reaction that then funnels itself toward, say, the pricier cosmetic counters – a stampede of frenzied shoppers seeking to smell good at 10 percent of the original cost. You simply can't yell that through a bullhorn. Ankle sprains and lost children in cases like that can really cut into a store's closely watched sales charts, because of involvement by security and first aid people. And it creates a field day for shoplifters and gropers.

To reduce the sales slippages that result, all the big stores have quietly adopted a standard system of silent signals, borrowed from the army.

In cases of security threats, stomping with the left heel creates a guttural wave of sound that sensors can track to its starting point. Starting a fist fight in men's colognes, for example, would summon floor detectives with a subdued rumble – and the other crowds of shoppers would be none the wiser.

Now here is a collection of observed signals and how to recognize trouble, even though you are an innocent bargain hunter.

All employees stand with hands clasped, as in prayer. (**Here comes the personnel manager.**)

A group clucking noise that is produced when store employees stimulate their lower palates with a curved tongue. (**Stampede in the free pimple clinic**)

Vertical arm signals with the fists pressed against the ribs, much like geese taking flight. (**Teenagers are cutting photos from pornographic magazines.**)

With arms extended, employees make their right palms rotate 180 degrees. (**A shoplifter has taken an assembled bicycle and is riding down the aisles in search of an exit.**)

Employees light long wooden matches and raise them above their heads, slowly making small overhead circles. (**Either a small child or a large fat person is contributing flatulence to the air conditioned, ozone-controlled environment.**)

Two female employees are running down the store aisles, waving towels over their heads with both hands. (**It's ladies choice after work in the men's shower room.**)

Some famous signals from history

Over the years, some signals have become legendary in the retail trade. In 1865 New York, snapping fingers announced the end of the U.S. Civil War and the return of cotton clothes from the South. In the 1920s, a chorus of spitting sounds originated when love god Rudolf Valentino got married. In the 1930s, earthy female war whoops greeted the daily arrival of Chicago gangster Al Capone, but as these were clearly vocal, they never made the official list.

If you see these signals today, never get involved. Diving at a waving person in a store still constitutes an assault under the Criminal Code and even then, it might be mistaken for an obscure signal meaning (**Cooties on the floor!**)

Also, try to be alert for undercover security officials, such as females posing as mannequins in the lingerie section. (**The giveaway clue: mannequins are never that squat in shape and they never wear brassieres under their peignoirs.**)

Persons impersonating store employees can be detected immediately, once you tell them, "It's your lunch break!" If they don't break into a dash to the elevator, they're fake employees and up to no good.

PART TWO

24.   Running With the Buffalo

Dave B. is in no way the kind of adolescent that teenaged girls would think of as cute. But for some females in a less polite society, he is a great reason to give off scent.

For up to two years, Dave has run with a herd of American bison across the Alberta plains, having been adopted by them as a privileged alien. Most herds will not take this extraordinary step for insurance reasons. In fact, no one would have learned of his life among the calves if it had not been for a PBS camera crew that was following a pack of wolves intent on feeding on his hosts. The wolves had given up in disgust when they noticed Dave among the calves.

Dave quietly dropped out of Dunnville & District Secondary School a few years ago and never even thought of American bison until he saw a big herd from the window of the bus he'd been riding to Vancouver.

In a rare interview, Dave said that initially, life with the buffalo herd was distasteful, even to him. "There was this awful smell, but once they got over mine, we were friends." He is a stocky young man and not the sort of teenager that would be accepted and promoted by the Air Cadets. Even though his hair is shoulder length and he has a premature belly, he can run as fast and as long as the average cow calf.

What attracted him and eventually induced him to stay with the herd was the acceptance he received from the female calves. "I never got that far with girls in school and with these calves, I've never had to put up with their smart back talk. I think they go for me because their mothers think I'm stupid and harmless. So, it's a win-win situation." Also, buffalo eyesight is notoriously poor.

Dave's thoughts on his new life on the plains are recorded here.

Personal Cleanliness
He says it's near impossible to avoid getting dirty, especially while running. If he steps in a cow patty while involved in a strenuous sprint, he simply keeps running and eventually his feet will get cleaned in the luxuriant grasses. Also, he makes doubly sure his foster family will never have to step in his.

Clothing for All Seasons

In the warm summer months, Dave wears a home-made loin cloth woven together with long grasses. In time, it turns to straw and can be discarded if he is far enough away from the public highways. He can make a new one in a day or two, but it takes longer to weave if he is running. He says, "What makes clothes like mine hard at times is when the bees start to swarm and they nest in the back of me. I don't mind and it sort of tickles, but it really stings when I sit down."

In the frigid winter months, Dave often keeps warm by snuggling close to his foster mother. He calls her Mudder and claims she's often called him Mister Bee. Once, at a bison cemetery, she presented Dave with a set of prosthetic horns that he wears to this day. Straw loin cloths won't do in the January cold snaps, so he changes into toasty-warm newspapers impregnated with cow spittle and moulted buffalo fur. For Dave, it's a sign of high status among the buffalo.

As far as the herd is concerned, Dave is a quality assurance engineer, a title respected by the bulls. The only names they have are written on monitoring tags installed by the scientists three years ago. Their names include Gonzo, Elmo, Smooger and Slimer, among others. Dave's tag is actually from the chrome on a Honda Civic. The bulls don't know, but it reads 'EX-L, inspected by quality assurance engineers'.

Dave's Diet
While the typical buffalo herd subsists on prairie grasses, Dave often can get creative. He seeks out succulent herbs during the warmer months and digs for ground hogs in winter. Local police also suspect he takes unsold pizzas from lonely prairie dumpsters.

Buffalo Sports
A favorite pastime among all buffalo is wallowing.

Buffalo Religious Practices
Many buffalo kneel down before digging holes in the snow. Anthropologists have long held that this is a link with a pre-millennial religion that accepted any outward signs of piety.

Buffalo Crime and Punishment
For all members of a buffalo herd, crime is not known, recognized or recorded. Dave said that on one occasion, he was punished. "I think one of the cows was offended by my casual hugging practices and struck me with her foot, right between the horns."

25. Advice to Young Ladies

Many young people, girls in particular, believe that accumulated wisdom happened when three or four soothsayers started writing it down: they got the giggles while writing, from passing around a gin bottle.

But Honor Phaapp, R.N., has some sober words to young ladies of the modern age. From her own experience and that of her contemporaries, she has codified "the best advice possible" and distilled it into a dozen important points.

She explained, "It falls somewhere between street smarts and common sense. There is a right and a wrong in every difficult situation and if you know it beforehand, you are better off every time." So here are Mrs. Phaapp's 12 points.

1. **Should I Always Check out My Roommate?**
   You never can be too sure of the person you are living with. Even people married for 50 years suspect the other of occasional axe assault. One dead giveaway that still manages to fool people is this housing request – "If you let me live at your place, I'll always leave when you come home and return when you leave." It sounds innocent enough, but sooner or later, the day will come when you return home from work and the roommate won't let you in. So don't be fooled by that request.

2. **How can You Blow Your Nose Without a Kleenex?**
   Always curl your left hand and turn away. After blowing your nose a couple of good times, excuse yourself and reach into your pocket. It's much like butting a cigarette onto a quarter, then putting the ashes into the cuff of your trousers. If your clothes have no cuffs, sew some onto the bottom of your skirt, shorts or culottes.

3. **Should I Rescue a Beached Whale?**
   Possibly, but first make sure it is a whale. You never know. Sometimes a shark will roll over sideways, hide its distinctive dorsal fin and wait for an innocent person to help. Next, check for smells; if the whale really stinks, it's dead and in no further need of rescue. Call the conservation police or boy scouts for its removal.

4. **Do cats and dogs go to heaven?**
   No. But they are better off if they have jobs.

5. **Is My Boyfriend About to Break Up With Me?**
   Keep an accurate record of his calls. Also, start checking his stories – does he always show up for work at his law firm, or does he work at the car wash where you usually meet. What has he bought you lately, apart from breath mints. Has he stopped shaving for dates? Check out the signs.

6. **I've stopped writing to my mother. Is that okay?**
   Probably. Always remember that she doesn't expect much. But if she lives close, like in the next bedroom, a polite nod often goes down well.

7. **If I avoid walking on cracks, you know, to save my mother's back, am I mental?**
   Maybe, but don't worry. Your physical fitness and coordination while walking will always balance things off.

8. **Can I have an Allowance?**
No.

9. **Last Night I Rolled Over and the Bag in my Waterbed Broke. What Next?**
This is 235 gallons of water and it weighs 2,000 pounds. Give notice to the landlord and leave quickly, if there are apartments downstairs.

10. **I Was In a Head-on Collision and the Gear Shift Went Right Through Me.**
Next time wear a seat belt. If it happens at your house, never dance while holding auto parts.

11. **I Have Facial Blemishes. Are they Contagious?**
It depends. Yes, they are catching if the marks are from measles or chicken pox. No, if you haven't changed razor blades and won't leave your face alone.

12. **I can't think of anything to ask right now.**
Good. The trick is – never let on.

26. Advice for Young Gentlemen

How to Siphon Gasoline
Say you can afford to make the installments on your car, but not pay for the gasoline. The first thing is to obtain two lengths of garden hose, one long and one short, from your mother if possible. Find an unoccupied, immobile car and open the gas cap. Insert the long hose into the gas tank and stick the other end into a waiting gas can. Insert the shorter hose into the gas tank and begin blowing. The gasoline will flow down the long hose and into the can. Sometimes the gasoline will spill onto your lower face, usually if you inhale. Never attempt this if you are wearing a moustache. One half will always fall off, but your breath will smell better.

The Theory of Relative Industry
You can get first-class grades in university by knowing only half the work. By knowing half of the work, you will have rubbed up against 25 percent of the rest and, by osmosis, you will have become familiar with 15 percent more. That adds up to 90 percent. You may now proceed to get your degree by mail order.

How to Raise Money in a Hurry
You have several options. The first is to hide next to the dumpster behind your neighborhood pizza place and wait until they throw out all their unsold pizza pies. Neatly arrange the slices in a clean box and sell them to senior citizens at a discount.

Put on a cardboard sign that warns of impending doom. Take a collection.

Buck Toothed Girls Always Get Married First

If you had known this sooner, you would have selected Mary Agnes Smelt much sooner. Also, had she known this, her father could have saved thousands on orthodontia. For some reason, bucktoothed maidens drive men crazy right away.

Dumpster Diving

If caught at it, just stand up, face the accusers and ask, "What? What?" Then go back to legitimate research until they leave. If you find something of value, as in money, keep silence. If someone lowers the lid on you, push up. If not, shut up. The next cost accountant passing by will always take a look and raise the lid.

Always Pause for Ladies

When out walking, you come to an intersection with stop signs and a lady drives up – always pause to let her go by. Not only is it polite, but nine out of 10 times, a lady driver will wait until you are in the crosswalk, then gun her engine. Maybe you look like a threat.

How to Impress a Girl

Never show her portrait once you have taken it. She will always demand a re-shoot. Publish the photo and demand she sit still the next time. Otherwise, forget trying to impress. You are hooped by now anyway.

Play Piano in a Night Club

Admit to knowing how, but never attempt it actually, unless the orchestra is really loud. Then sit facing the audience. Play either 'Chopsticks' or 'Old McDonald Had a Farm'. While you play, emit loud yowls of atmospheric joy – pretentious, but attractive to various drunks.

How to be Cool

Don't go anywhere until someone rips your heart out. Then wait until you finish crying. Practice, in front of a mirror, the art of keeping your expression blank for hours at a time. Turn up your collar; if you don't have one, turn up your sleeves. Practice saying, "Ah, jeez!" over and over. Those seeking recognition will love you for it.

When to Stop Frying Food

You may stop frying your food when it stops making all that noise.

There is a Jackass in Every Workplace

It happens with every job. A key figure inhabits your office, warship or worship and turns out to be demented, a micromanager or a combination of both. Furthermore, he or she will have some blood or carnal relationship with the boss. The supreme lesson is this: stand up to this bully or not, he/she will always leave the company's employ shortly after you do; never before.

27. Dressing Tips for Men

If you insist on dressing yourself and purchasing your wardrobe alone and untutored in retail stores, you ought to consider some basic rules of men's dress. The result would be a life free of public embarrassment, as well as an actual uptick to your self-esteem.

Suits

To begin with, there are two basic rules for suits – those designed for portly, middle aged men and shaped much like a church bell – and those for males ages 16 to 29 with builds like aphids made out of pipe cleaners. If you wear a two-piece suit tailored for a young man, you will find your entire body trying to squeeze upwards and out of it, like a butterfly climbing limp and wet from its cocoon. These are best left to the young bank clerks of Korea or Hong Kong, who live on rice diets and have builds inherited from generations of male waifs.

Instead, copy the styles worn by politicians. Their jackets are fuller, longer and reeking of power. While a well-tailored Asian pant leg will draw women like moths, suggestions of power will drive them to a happy frenzy.

Ties

Avoid ties that make you look like a felon just escaped from the gallows. No matter the reason, some men are addicted to skinny ties that hang from their adam's apple straight down like a single pin stripe. Instead, put on ties that show that you know haberdashery from skateboarding.

Shirts and Underwear

There are many grave sins that pass unnoticed in our streets today – invisible, that is, until the men wearing them remove their jackets and begin working. Whether you like it or not, the image of authentic power is service and like nowhere else, the workplace is the milieu for showing your stuff.

Make sure all your shirt buttons are in place and even better, that your shirts fit. They must remain tucked into your pant waist and they should fit around your belly. Otherwise, they reveal your underwear, and all too often, it should be termed *under-awfuls*.

There is a main fashion secret for men to be followed here: Copy the women. It's taken them centuries to achieve it, but women have the unmentionables knocked.

Here are their rules:

1. Never wear colored underwear under white shirts.
2. Keep shirts loose and undies tight.
3. Never let anyone see skin – or underwear waists - from your navel to your knickers.
4. Change your undies with each work shift.

Accessories

Sweat bands: We owe a lot to the men of antiquity, because the innovations they inspired still remain with us today. One of them is the head band. Invented by the hard working fishers and thieves of Sardinia, a tightly tied sweatband, or strip of absorbent cloth, keeps the sweat of your brow from entering your eyes and turning them a beet red.

However, wearing a simple sweatband does not protect your eyes from stupidity. If you have to tie it to fit your skull, always wear it above your eyes and never let the knot and its loose ends dangle in front of the eyes. They go toward the rear end of your melon. Worn in front, they become more than a simple sight hazard, but proclaim you everywhere as a criminal dimwit.

Kilts: No these were not invented by Scotsmen running commando through their native glens; these actually came from the Middle East and were adopted by such famous operatives as Julius Caesar and King Solomon. One recently discovered pottery shard shows King Solomon standing in front of an adoring crowd with a manly swelling in the front of his kilt. Undoubtedly it refers to his wives and 700 concubines, not for having them, but for keeping them busy.

Modern admirers of these ancient figures would do well to emulate them. Rather than leaping naked from the shower on your wedding night and scaring the bejaysus out of your bride, it would be better to walk slowly, in a kilt, toward her in the half light and beckoning her to some new – or well-practiced - delights.

Corsets: These days, having a butler fasten the laces of your girdle from behind you simply does not occur. Instead, your unsightly fat is whipped out of you by an assortment of medical routines, including liposuction.

The financially strapped gentlemen who wish to avoid such rough play with their midsections are urged to consider turning the corsets around and lacing them up themselves. Here, they save untold labor invoices from domestic servants, as well as embarrassing medical fees.

28.   The Exciting Uses of Disinfectant

There is nothing fresher than the scent of alcohol when you are feeling grungy. All lazy notions flee away and you are actually ready to face whatever comes each day. But in case you need a disinfecting and you are not in a convenient location, you should check out the following methods available to you when the smell of alcohol would not be appreciated, as in church or in a courtroom.

Ultrasonic cleaning trends

This method of cleansing has been around for more than 50 years and it's generally used for cleaning medical equipment. However, no stretch of the imagination can bar you from using it, as long as your personal needs revolve around cables, electronic parts and ceramics. So if you are among the growing number of people who use bionic limbs, or who are about to insert semiconductors into their bodies, a quick check of suppliers is a good thing. Nothing is worse than applying alcohol or soap to an android's head.

Protocols for Cleaning Children

Children are a completely different thing, unless you suspect an individual child is possessed by the Devil or other phenomena. If you see flashing lights behind your child's eyes, the first thing to do is detect his battery source. This may most often be found in the child's backpack. In the main, washing can then be done with soap and vigorous scrubbing. However, if soap causes the child to fade in and out of your vision, and if levitation occurs, you can apply the same ultrasonic equipment you would use to clean jewellery or digital appliances.

The Bodily Fluid Exchange Cleanup Kit

Chance encounters with bodily fluids can be disarming to say the least. If an employee suddenly throws up in a company meeting, the situation is best handled by donning personal protective equipment (PPE) before taking any direct action.

The first action to take is ordering all other employees to keep a 30-foot radius away from the discommoded employee. All of their affected clothing should be removed immediately and sent out for a cleaning process that involves scalding hot water. If any employee needs to take a bus home, he or she should be issued white coveralls that can be returned the next day. A simple flushing with a fire extinguisher should take care of the employee who has hurled.

All present should put on face masks with shields and goggles, covers for their shoes, disposable gowns over their clothes and each should don a pair of disposable, non-absorbent medical-grade gloves.

The employee who has hurled should be doused with kitty litter and then wrapped in lengths of paper towels. No smoking should be permitted at this time.

In the meantime, the expelled bodily fluids should be cleaned up and all employees in the room then should remove all of their clothing, to prepare for the appropriate management inspection.

Googles and face masks are normally exempt from this stage of investigation and follow-through.

Optional Uses for PPE

If any employee so requests, PPE may be allowed for personal use on weekends, unless an employee has a reputation for weird costumes at friend parties. But if a manager believes the request is serious, as in discreet bathing for church baptisms, or on first dates, it is better to err on the side of caution in the prevention of bodily fluid exchange.

In an Emergency

If you are seated in a public place and you believe you may have come in contact with fleas, head lice or intrusive pets, the careful use of matches or portable acetylene torches may be allowed. Burning of animals, while generally frowned on in public, may be just the thing to discourage future contact. Ultrasonic cleansing equipment may work on infection sources that are sensitive to touch. The use of tasers on exposed skin areas in large crowds is approved of, but only with the proper training.

General Observations and Cautions

While many medical professionals may use ultrasonic hand buzzers for frivolous pranks, their repeated use is discouraged by the authorities. More than three uses is generally a red flag, when used on one victim alone. Medical training and supervision are required in cases where such procedures as hair transplants and new moustaches are applied to sleeping vendors or vagrants. The best rule of thumb is this: less is more, except in haste.

29.   F = AP: Suction and the World of Tomorrow

Many people have tried to figure out their bathroom plungers over the years, to no good effect. It's all due to suction and the formula $F = AP$ applies here. F is the force used. A is the area over which the plunger, or suction cup, is applied. P is the atmospheric pressure outside the cup. But now, the humble FAP principle promises new horizons for the entrepreneurial scientist.

Many areas of dire human need will be addressed by the brave new world of suction, to a degree never before imagined.

Convenience in the world of high fashion

No one ever talks about it, but the plain truth is that many skinny runway models experience the unpleasantness of droopy and falling trousers when they stride down the fashion runway. "Holding up trousers on skinny models" is the new mission statement of the Sewanee Institute, according to spokesman Dr. Amos Phaap.

Teams of Dr. Phaap's students are hard at work finding stronger suction cups to apply to the waistbands of skinny-minny slacks. One of the best comes with peanut butter smeared on the insides. The touchy part is peeling it off and super strong Irishmen are being recruited to do the job with spatulas. So far, the models are refusing all help. Dr. Phaap has signalled he needs more time and is recruiting in Texas now.

Travels in Outer Space

Have you ever dreamed of zooming from Earth to Jupiter at a speed far greater than with conventional rocket engines? Some day you will go so fast they will have to set new time standards. The only thing holding up this tremendous advance in space travel is figuring out how to stop your propelling body when it reaches its destination. Right now, they can fire you off to Jupiter, but once you arrive, robots will have to scrape you off the Jupiter airport wall.

Law, Order and the Punishment of Criminals

You break the law and society will fix you. First, a giant plunger will suck you out of your hideout, because at birth you will have been implanted with a GPS sensor to guide it. In prison, you will be glued to a wall for decades at a time. And your execution will see you imploded into a limp cube by four reverse plungers, before you are shot through a big straw to the jello yard.

If Gravity Attracted Vacuum...

It's one of the best high school insults – if gravity attracted vacuum, you'd be standing on your head. Well, that day has come. Fail in school and you will be transferred to Sewer Central, where teams of low IQ employees are lowered into manholes to extract blockages.

Henry VIII and the Reformation

England's repellant King Henry VIII created more than he bargained for when he applied excessive suction. He was in the closing stages of an illicit romance with one of his older mistresses when he tried kissing her long and hard. She enjoyed it until his massive lips sucked out her upper partial and got stuck in his. Words led to words, an archbishop or two was fired and she lost her monthly income. And all the Catholics in England had to give up their false teeth on Fridays.

Advances in Gourmet Cookery

Pulled pork sandwiches, invented in the deepest South, have swept the country and those parts of the world where pig meat is okay to eat. Now, the same inventive knowhow has produced the pulled baloney sandwich, which is okay to eat even in kosher and Arab countries. A mechanized, super plunger automatically removes unhealthy bits of proteins, then assembles the good ones and lays them out in six-inch strings. These are fried into batches by the thrifty consumer and spread on cheese bagels before consumption.

The reverse plunger concept is used to create suction milk shakes, grilled cheese concentrate and seared *grouper en croute glacee*. The last one is a dense fish that is served after being blown through a tube and encased in freshly created glass. You cannot eat a grouper this way, but you are allowed to be fascinated as it swims around inside the glass.

New Hope for Wildlife

For far too long, the big predators in nature – the sharks, grizzly bears and muggers – have generally had their way. Those species that are lower on the food chain have been at the mercy of these big bullies for millions of years. Now, biologists have been active in attaching radioactive suction cups on the snouts of these predators. The cups send signals to their fellows and generally, shark fixes onto shark, grizzly onto grizzly, and mugger onto pimp – and so on. It renders them less able to attack when they are joined together.

What is means for the rest of the un-picturesque members of biology is that more of the victims will survive. In time, bacteria could form on the skins of less active predators and slowly eat them up. And if species of krill, salmon and poor humans can appreciate it in time, they will have more stability in their lives.

30.   Special Folk Who Enriched Our Lives

All my life I have remembered Uncle Dwayne who was so bald. If he stood against a certain light, you could see the gold fish swimming around inside his head. He was a special man who never starved and in his honor, I wish to present others like him today. They were the best potash and cow manure for the human matrix.

Herbert Thmiele
He might have become renowned as a quality breeder of horses and yet, he spent his entire business career as the breeder and trainer of the Lipizzaner Burros. He started off with the aim of preparing these cute little equines for performances in midget circuses, but when recessionary times impacted that branch of show business, he turned to landscape maintenance. People these days who desire sustainable lifestyles prefer the burros on their lawns to mowers. The Thieles ate only three burros any given winter.

Deptford J. Tilbury
Possibly the best exemplar of what is finest in journalists, Mr. Tilbury only spent three years behind bars. On a bet, he had tried to live a week's normal life while being pursued by paparazzi. Casting a knowing eye on his fellow writers, he commented, "When we begin to moralize, it's time to lock up the silver."

Father Alexei Zhukob
The pastor of St. Herman of Alaska parish in suburban Duluth, he was renowned for taking a blind man and making him deaf. Many other such miracles were attributed to him, but he shied away from all publicity.

Mme. Vakawaka

A practitioner of Haitian voodoo, Miss Vakawaka was arrested many times in her life, but never convicted of the crimes people accused her of. On one occasion, she was accused of causing a man to jump from a high bridge. On another, she was suspected of poisoning only the male blowfish in her aquarium. Locally, she was famous not for her spiritual abilities, but for failing to persuade all local men to marry her.

Lt. Col. Louis Marie Villewipp

One of Napoleon Bonaparte's more audacious aides, Villewipp was found hiding in a well after the Battle of Moscow; he had been frozen to the bottom and his echoed cries were heard by the whole army. It was rumored he was so stupid, even the sailors noticed.

Mrs. Esmee Miph

While she never intended to become noticed, Mrs. Miph gained fame by refusing - always - to fasten her seat belt. She complained it always wrinkled her clothes. Once, when thrown by the force of impact through her car's windshield, she became impaled on the gear shift. She attributed the resultant scar to soccer practice with some attractive men.

Tri-Moxie Siddle

Named after an important dream by her mother, Ms. Siddle became an adept feminist and was credited with taking a whole truck load of dry cement mix and dumping it into a male-only swimming pool. After the immediate outcry, police realized it was winter, the pool was empty and the cement could be re-used for constructing a wholly female cell block, just for her.

Private Eurekus Bidden

Probably the most reviled traitor of the American Revolution, he had been inspired by his hero, General Benedict Arnold, who defected to the British with some important plans. Private Bidden became confused by watch signals and defected to General George Washington, his own commanding officer. Refusing all offers of clemency, he was taken to a frozen duck pond and installed there for good.

Last of the Deemsters

Word has arrived of the passing of Lachlan Pethewey, of Loch Duntroon, Scotland, last of the world's deemsters. His death marked the final curtain on the influence of deemsters, who rendered acute judgement on many aspects of social life, until the emergence of government-paid teachers. The deemsters were direct descendants of the Doomsters, a macabre sort of Scottish executioner. When those judges, hangmen and torturers disappeared in the face of legal liberalization, the deemsters carried on their arch-conservative ways. The final judgement of Mr. Deemster Pethewey was that rock and roll music was "deemed" not necessarily satanic, as long as it was played on the tin whistle. His rulings were quoted in many laughable newspapers, who accepted his "deemed proper" rulings without question or research.

31.   Wearable Tech Appliances

Now that our military has authorized soldiers to enter the battlefield with implanted cloaking devices, we have been able to terrorize the Arabs for a change. And now, it has opened the floodgates to a surprising assortment of commercial innovations. War has always been the mother of gadgets.

Personal Hygiene

With brand new safeguards in place, implanting personal hygiene products into our bodies, instead of applying those products to our tired old skins, has become a reality. For example, with enzymes that automatically flow to our feet and clean them, we no longer have to subject our heels and toes to cold bathroom floors. All we have to do is empty the blister-pack packages, insert them in our shoes for a day and the new system works seamlessly. Now, a modern person needs only to wash himself from the ankles up, eliminating the bother of bending over or sitting down to achieve clean feet. The cleaning residue is absorbed naturally into one's socks. One still has to make sure the correct product is used, because the tooth-brushing kit may actually harm the feet with its built-in abrasives, and laundering panty hose containing toothpaste may cause washing machine back-ups.

Birth control implants, while still controversial, are best left to the medical professionals. This is because doctors and nurses have accommodated themselves to the few available product stocks.

The Body and Haute Cuisine

There is nothing like a hot cup of coffee each morning. The new technology has made it easier to dispense with those annoying and messy plastic pods that contain single servings of specialty coffees and cocoa. The wearable "Caffe Belt" worn during the night around the waist, brings water to the boiling point for your favorite blend, and then infuses it when the contents of the belt are squeezed into a demitasse. You can drink your joe without moving a single toe out of bed. Marital relations are discouraged while the belts are being worn. Smoking is optional.

More people are investing their savings in prosthetic slow cookers. Before leaving home for the office each morning, people are quietly stoking their cookers with cuts of roasting beef, spices, vegetables and rice. These are discreetly worn on the chest and safely contained in composite materials that use body heat to cook the dinner food during the day, without setting fire to one's clothes. Instead of worrying about their food cooking at home, office and factory workers can check it by opening heavy plastic windows, in the privacy of their cubicles.

Secret Compartments

It's no secret that the expensive briefcases and backpacks you see on the subway and bus each day contain lunches and snacks only. The real reason people spend hundreds of dollars on this work-related luggage is because they are supposed to take important business papers home, for extra work. Plastic surgery has progressed to a point now which allows more personal intrusions. Instead of breast and buttock enhancements, many women and men are opting for polite portfolios that are hidden in the folds of the skin.

While the traditional briefcase still carries the sandwiches and brownies, the hidden portfolios carry discreet papers and the occasional breath mint.

It is true that larger people may contain more ample storage and the loss prevention officers of all retail stores must be alert for shoplifters who are larger when they leave than when they enter.

Medical Gems

An exciting inroad into the weight loss industry has been made by specialists who have married the technologies of vacuum cleaners and nano-liposuction in the new Slim-Style Vacation Packages. While people take a long weekend trip to Mexico, the machines remove unwanted fatty deposits. The customers merely swallow large 'grapes' containing the working parts and return home at half their original size.

Few things are more embarrassing than the sudden collapse of noses and other body parts when cosmetic surgery is not updated. Lush lips can swiftly become puckered droops and so, the new lines of Instant Tuck Technologies Inc. can help. Simply place the packaged gel over the embarrassing body part and it swiftly adjusts to provide the needed support. If the wearer forgets or is too lazy to check in with the cosmetic surgeon, a loud siren starts sounding and will not stop until the first down payment is made to the receptionist at surgery.

Vertigo is a scourge and a menace to everyone. Implanted sensors instruct the inner ear to 'smarten up' if a person is starting to lean over too far while walking. Researchers are still working to replace the loud beeping noise that emits from the nose, with silent warnings.

32.   Choirs for Hire

People have enjoyed listening to massed choirs for centuries. Most often, they are a part of religious services, as conduits to a mighty rise in spirits just before the offerings are asked. But increasingly in our troubled times, they are taking on a notorious reputation.

In history, however, there is a balanced view and a better experience. Choral music, or "goat song", got its big chance at fame in the classical Greek theater. The Romans were no slouches in the music department either and they became known for their performances at the funerals of rich people. Normally, a choir would proclaim the goodness and greatness of such worthies as Nero and Caligula, and then watch as their performances were followed by the deadly gladiatorial games.

Our main impressions of choirs have come either from church, or from the soundtracks of famous movies. You can always tell the good guys from the bad when you see the heroes go to their deaths. As they bow before the executioner's axe, the camera lens slowly rises from their scaffold scenes to the heavens, as a choir sings: mainly in vowels. The deaths of villains follow, accompanied by short grunts on a saxophone. Then real life continues, with no music.

In today's shifting world, the work of choirs is nothing if not commercial. Here are a few.

The Scat-Song Choir

Mostly heard during television commercials, this choir is known as the most venerable, not because of its age, but for the length of its residual royalty payments. Believe it or not, the only lyrics it ever uses are these – "Scooby-Do, scooby-do, scooobie!"

If you listen closely, you can tell what they're up to. The use of 'scooby-do' with a brisk, lilting cadence bestows an impression on the listener right away: it signifies the wondrous thing your life will become if you buy and use their product. However, "Scooby-do" can mean murderous things, as in when it is sung with a long, low-octave under-murmur of "Uh Oh"; like, there's a big blizzard tonight. And who can resist the tug and pull of "Scooby-do" when it is sung like the spirituals of the deep South, as when Republicans run for office.

The Orphan Boys Choir

Here is another use of choral music without consonants or syllables. Accompanied by a jaw harp or a kazoo, the music rises and dips like a great school of herring. Nothing stands in the way of these competent voices that are aimed at the very gills and snouts of our remote emotions. Using this choir, the most homely man can instantly conquer the most intimidating maiden.

As an example, the Trojan Prince Paris used such an unbeatable choir when he wooed – and won – Helen. The wife of Greek King Menelaus, she became Helen of Troy and inspired 50,000 intrepid soldiers to their deaths. All done with a bass kazoo, a tenor jaw harp and a nasal sounding Greek letter E.

The Loo Loo Choir

Watch out for these guys. They have appeared in movies for decades, usually as the backup voices of such Hollywood greats as Bing Crosby, Errol Flynn and Sophia Loren. Much like the

Scooby-Do gang, these pre-puberty sharpsters can guarantee the actor an immediate association with divinity and heavenly purity, with limited lyrics – "Loo, loo, looo.".

They first appeared with Crosby in sentimental films like "Going My Way" and sang with alarming persuasion in the great cathedral scene from "The Pride and the Passion". A huge cannon is being pulled into the church by a suddenly pristine mob of Spanish guerilleros and the whole place is ablaze with undeniable truth. They are going to win. (Actually, they do, but poor Ms. Loren is mowed down later by the sneering French.)

Back-Up Singers
Have you ever wondered where these wondrous marvels come from? For many years, soloists with the strongest voices have used backup singers with telling effect. You never know their names, but three or four men or women in ensemble provide one of the most convincing displays of unbeatable persuasion, no matter how smarmy the press and courts have revealed the soloists to be.

There is nothing so undefeated in the inner soul as the emotion that rises when a singer ruined by life, is backed up by an ensemble of beautiful people who simply adore him. And again, their lyrics are simply vowels, or repetitions of his. Alone, he would have been pathetic. With them, the audience sits back, smiles and imagines life alone in his arms.

33.   The Wainfleet Fairies

The strange case of the Wainfleet Fairies was opened by the Dunnville police many years ago after a group of small children walked into a country church one Sunday morning and announced they wanted to make a donation.

They placed small gifts into an offering basket and silently walked out of the front door. Their 'gift' turned out to be small slices of a sweet cake and several tiny objects of gold – spheres less than one inch wide, earrings, bracelets and signet rings.

This was repeated a week later and one of the strange children was heard to say the gifts were from the "fairies". Members of the congregation, an independent bunch that believed in beards and bonnets, walked after them and watched as they disappeared down the road.

Throughout that summer, in 1850, the fascinating event was repeated many times. Gold pieces were distributed to families of the congregation and in time, word of it spread in the surrounding counties. A policeman was assigned to investigate.

The Case is Opened

The officer in question, Danton Goupil, attended the church twice before the visitors appeared again. They showed up the third time he was there and made the same announcement as before: "If it please you, we will forward come and gifting make." Goupil, who moments before had been dreaming about the blonde lady in the front row, noticed quickly the almost medieval-Tudor way the visitors spoke. Moreover, they were all blonde, about three feet tall, with one of them bearing a leather bag. She emptied the jingling bag into the offering basket, stepped back and turned to face the congregation. The rest gathered with her and began in soprano voices to sing:

"Ole, ole,. ole, ole, ole, ole, ole, ole, ole, ole, ole, ole, ole, ole, ole, ole, ole, ole."

As they sang, a great peace came over everyone in the church. Goupil moved closer to the blonde lady and she held his hand for a long time. Everyone was in a trance, a golden glow of love. But as they left, the policeman remembered his assignment and quietly followed them. Out they went and down the road they walked, with the officer in quiet pursuit.

He could hear them chatter as they walked. One said, "Maybe we should have done "Maria, I just met a girl named Maria?" No matter. They all merged swiftly into a stand of elm trees to the right of the road and disappeared. Goupil searched for several hours but could find nothing, except some scorched grasses in a clearing. The visitors never returned.

The Inquiry is Conducted
In the months and years that followed, all sorts of worthy people stepped forward with offers of help. The Anglican church dispatched a team of exorcists. John Brown, the great abolitionist of Kansas, came with a huge troop of cavalry and scoured the woods, setting them afire with their southern cigars. Child welfare leaders descended from all civilized cities and staged a teach-in, before vanishing. The general opinion of all those worthies was that the entire visit experience was either a mass delusion of the little church and its leaders, or it was an authentic mystery. If it was a mystery, they announced, local people would be allowed to rope off the little church as an historic site and charge admission.

Goupil and the blonde lady vanished as well and were rumored to have lived their lives in quiet magnificence somewhere else.

General consensus today is the only measurement of those strange and enchanting days. It runs thus – a group of pre-teens from Roswell, N.M., found a strange craft, took it for a weekend joyride and returned the same night with shrugs and whistling. In the end, it all amounted to an extra-terrestrial prank. It will be repaid when NASA gets its technology together.

No movies were made of this and no books were written. But every time someone in Wainfleet turns on the radio or television, little golden balls rise into the air all over the place and yodel like drunken sparrows.

34.   Rust Belt Renaissance

Wherever people live, they generally tend to repeat themselves. Using ancient Troy on the Dardanelles as an example, archaeologists swear they have found the remains of seven ancient cities, all built on the ruins of the first. Many famous cities place their trust in foundations built on the past, London for example, and Paris.

It is no surprise therefore that brash, new architectural enterprises (They are right on top of old industrial plants) are sprouting up like weeds across the civilized world. (In the uncivilized world, no photographs are permitted, but it is generally surmised that forests still hide the kinkiest temples.)

Where old factories from the Industrial Revolution employed thousands of poor men and women and belched out black smoke day and night, gentrified condominiums now attract wealthy buyers. The old brick and stone iron works that once supplied cannon for the Civil War now house digital research and development companies that seek to make our lives even better.

Any renaissance is better thought of as a frequent awakening after dark decades of sameness; instead of a glorious time in history, where women poisoned their lovers and men wore long hair and tights.

Here is a random sampling of what you may encounter when you tour our cities, safely of course, from the second floor of a secure bus.

New Life for Old Sports Venues
Popular sports come and go. Where throngs of besotted Romans once cheered on the deadly skills of gladiators in huge arenas, new throngs of beer drinking spectators now cheer on ranks of helmeted football players in tights.

However, the ancient coliseums have been replaced by condos with common parks at their centers. Pretty enough in perspective, but on Sunday afternoons, the healing sleep of many hung-over condo dwellers is interrupted by the strident sound of marching bands, baton twirlers and peanut sellers as famous old marching bands still adhere to the terms of their ancient contracts. No one ever thought to cancel their contracts and these days, they have become a prized source of income for many. Notre Dame still marches on as do many other famous drum and bugle corps.

Industrial Connections To the Occult
The best part of an employee's day is spent toiling respectfully for a benevolent boss. However, life in the 19th Century foundries was anything but recreational and even though the interiors now house pleasing interiors to fit the careers of architects, hookers and other upscale professions, they are often plagued by visits from the previous work force.

It's no surprise to see the faces of Ebenezer Scrooge, Bob Cratchit and Isambard K. Brunel, when computer programmers take their coffee breaks. Like the toilers of today, the old boys wonder also what their work was really all about. Who's to blame them for another look?

Government of the Consented

If necessity is the mother of all invention, persistence then is the father: that's why little happens that is new. For centuries, governments have been looking for places to hide their reviled civil service workers. The permit seekers, it is believed, will give up their grim pursuits of project approval and submit in silence to the creaky wheels of government.

Tax authorities for centuries have been bastions of conservatism. Some in the collections branch still wear the grimy top hats their great grandfathers prized so much. (They still talk to the women whose daguerreotypes still smile inside the crowns.)

The Role of Food Sellers

To spare the residents of the new condos the stress of supermarkets, with their subliminal messages whispered over loudspeakers, and the jumble of packaged foods vying for attention, the new living zones now offer food vendors who walk through the streets, crying out their wares.

With the collapse of the bottled beverage industry, consumers have been allowed to operate their own distillation and collection schemes. Therefore, all condos have come equipped with optional hookups to breweries, wine vats and stills. Newfie Screech and Allegheny Knee Slapper are among the favorites.

Commuting Improvements

It's no surprise that people living in the new developments are hesitant to leave their homes each morning and go to work. With that trend in mind, military personnel enter the homes each morning and snap knotted cords to the bottom of all the hammocks. Sleepers are up and ready in no time.

The big change here was that, with all the advancements in entertainment nightly, none of the condo class was willing to go to bed. The hammocks replaced the more tiresome beds that had to be made each day.

35. Songs to Sing in a Crisis

Cutting edge technology now can provide us with holograms of famous figures, living and dead, for speaking to large or worried groups of people. Buddy Holly, the lead singer of the 1950s Crickets, can appear and bang out tunes on his guitar and Eva Peron, the former first lady of Argentina, can strut the same stage, walking down a ramp uttering intelligible messages and working the crowd into a froth.

More often than not, miraculous technology like that may not be available when needed. There may be a power failure. Worse than that, a thunder storm may be in progress, threatening who knows what and frightening the shorts off of good citizens.

The key to charming our fears into mumbled nothings is a good song, sounded properly, and a humble musical instrument.

For instance, you may be trapped in a mall, deprived of electricity, phone service and french fries and in rushes an entire company of frightened marines. They look to you for help. What to do?

Well, the first thing is to walk among them, bucking them up. Marines can be shy and so you have no room for visible trembling yourself. Nothing upsets a fighting man than the sight of a quivering chin and a trembling hand. He may think you know more than he does.

Stand up on a chair and first, call for silent prayer. Keep it long enough to include all faiths, especially the Pentecostals who tend to go the longest. Then, encourage them to sing along with you in unison. The piece de resistance is this: a kazoo, played with humility. It brings a note of humility to the proceedings.

Try a few verses of the "Ballad of Davy Crockett". Get the marines to walk in step, in a big circle, each person clasping the right shoulder of the person ahead. Really belt out the words in each chorus.

Next, fill the time with "99 Kilos of Wine on the Wall" and keep it going until the lights come on. Do not interrupt if an individual breaks into tears and wailing. We're all human. So delegate deputies for counselling on the spot.

Modern Songs for Modern Problems
The people in your condo see a group of people coming and panic. They have no way of knowing the arrivals are headed for an annual Christmas church pageant and are dressed in the bathrobes and head towels of Palestinian shepherds. With fake beards. As far as your fellow mortgage payers know, they are about to be confronted with Islamic terrorists, marching in two by two.

Nothing works better than a stout hearted song in cases like this. The Notre Dame Fight Song is a good bet, or the Zulu wedding song from "Shaka".

Nothing scares off terrorists with the knowledge that prepared troops with guns and big dogs are awaiting them. So while some of you do their best Rottweiler barks and whines, others can start the Zulu chant "U-suthu" in unison. Baritone and basses do the best here. Sopranos and contraltos are great at ululation that rises above the din.

In cases like this, weapons and the occasional running charge are unnecessary. Those terrorists will head for the nearest bus to Syria when they hear the first grunt.

Facing International Tensions
Gazing into your back yard, you notice that emissaries from a foreign nation have planted their flag in your lawn. They have claimed your land as "New Yemen" or "La Nouvelle France". They are setting up tents and cooking pots and very soon, they will take their ownership for

granted before moving into – your home. If you don't act quickly, you may become an historical footnote in many of their adventure tales.

The first thing to do is sound the kazoo. Play "Reveille" next and either phone the police or summon your lawyer. Start your lawn mower and begin advancing on the explorers slowly, in parallel lines. Put your best speakers on the lawn, turn up your CD player and repeatedly play the national anthem of Russia. Dazed and confused, the newcomers will try another planet.

36.   Cooking With Kleenex

The legacies of many ancient peoples have been submerged for millennia in the oceans of unrecorded history, but now archaeology has confirmed what singers of oral ballads have known since the beginning of time: wrapped parcels of food were once exchanged on pagan holidays by being passed quickly through a bonfire.

This has survived in the French practice of serving dishes *en flambe*. Until now, the connection has eluded scholars, but Dr. Amos Phapp, of the Sewanee Institute, said the earliest chefs of France had been influenced by the Thumm people of what is now Paris. These primitive fisher peoples flourished for centuries on the Isle de Paris and they kept alive the practice of tossing the food parcels, more as a romantic joke than a religious observance.

"They would wrap morsels of fish in dry grass and the idea was for engaged couples to return each toss as quickly as possible. The poets tell us of flaming morsels as thick as fireflies, flying across the Seine River on moonlit nights. Sometimes, they would set girls' hair on fire and sometimes, in the case of rejection, they would be hurled back by overhand," Dr. Phapp explained.

Over the millennia, wrapping food parcels with grass evolved into complicated folds of tissue paper. Dr. Phapp noted that the courting practice, for practical and legal reasons, has never been re-enacted.

Dishes are pronounced *en flambe* once they have been doused with brandy and then set alight. However, setting fire to a family dinner is a rare occurrence, because of the costs of brandy, so Kleenex has survived as a practical substitute.

Here is one medieval recipe: custard *en flambe*

Bring the custard to the boil. Pour into spherical molds. Let cool overnight in a refrigerator. The following evening, wrap them in Kleenex, preferably of the 'lotion' variety as it facilitates combustion, and furtively set each one aflame. Hurl.

Dr. Phapp suggests that an incident of this kind actually occurred at Dieppe, on the English Channel, and initiated the 100 Years War. Even so, mortality rates were quite high for the practitioners of this *battaille de feu*, so it died out quickly. However, some alert chemists used the principles of this recipe to create some of the most useful implements known to man: custard pies, hand grenadines, Molotov mocktails, exploding cannolis and custard balloons.

These became so popular that the French people, inventive as regular Martians, came up such practical jokes as short-sheeting the beds of honeymooners and filling bagpipes with delayed-action firecrackers.

In fact, the annals of the French resistance fighters of World War II are full of naughty tricks played on their Nazi oppressors. Most of them can be traced to their ancient Thumm ancestors.

Dr. Pfaapp reported that a common morale evaporator was hiding weeks-old fillets of fish inside the Panzer tanks. A common ruse was the anonymous Yuletide delivery of cow patties to S.S. officers, each 'gift' carefully wrapped in colored Kleenex.

Furthermore, a long-hushed-up practice of the Foreign Legion was to hide the latrines of their Arab foes and erect bogus outhouses made of elasticized rubber. These were known to cause post-traumatic stress disorder long before a battle even began.

"Such dirty tricks were invented by other ancient peoples," Dr. Pfaapp said. "There are examples of cow bladders sewn into whoopee cushions for placement in the tombs of the pharaohs, to scare off would-be grave robbers, to say nothing of the common English custom of inserting Alka Seltzer in one's afternoon tea. It was as if the Marx brothers worked at Downton Abbey."

37.   Great Moments in Industrial Archaeology

Through all the streams of world history, one central statement has endured: the private experiences of the rich are, well, none of our business; until now. Industrial archaeology has come of age.

In his final exit to the mists of Edwardian history, Carson the butler says to Lady Margaret, "Your breakfast burrito, milady. Bangers on the side." Now, archaeology experts sifting through the social debris at Downton Abbey have made a surprising discovery.

Chanticleer Phaap, uncle of Dr. Amos Phaap, of the Sewanee Institute, announced that in the old butler's pantry, his team has found evidence of corn meal and chickpeas. "Obviously, this was the site of an old bakery on an industrial scale. To feed such a large staff, the Downton executive had turned to Latin American processed food."

It explains Carson's disappearance in 1924. It seems the redoubtable senior servant had eloped to Mexico with Lady Margaret Crawley and invented the nacho.

In a similar vein, the discovered skeleton of English King Richard III has resulted in another revelation. Industrial spectronomy has established from the king's teeth that his diet shifted once he was crowned monarch, from merely rich dainties to an almost complete ingestion of wine. The stress of being an evil king, naughty or not, made him utter all sorts of bad sayings – enough to fill William Shakespeare's play and a few Marvel comics beside. The little king was a wino.

Stunning archaeological finds like this not only add needed glamor to the dusty life of old diggings, they give today's inquiring minds all sorts of mental granola to chew on.

Military Discoveries
The Battle of Kadesh in 1274 B.C. was a famous victory for the Egyptian Pharaoh Rameses II, partly because it involved more chariots than any other military campaign. It took place on the Orontes River in what is now Syria, with Rameses facing a much larger army of Hittite warriors. Whether Rameses won (or said he did) is immaterial now because excavations on the site have unearthed the remnants of a decisive weapon.

Fragments of metal and ceramics together, hidden beneath a huddle of Hittite skeletons have been put together and, for the first time, reveal the Hittites had developed a Bronze Age death ray. It seems the weapons, made in modern-day Turkey, were advanced enough to inflict catastrophic injuries on the Egyptians. However, Dr. Phaap says the battery technology had not developed sufficiently to allow long-term use. No batteries had evolved past the C-cell stage.

"The death ray failed, but not before it scared the hell out of the Egyptians," Dr. Phaap said. "They retreated home telling everyone an angel of fire had barred their way. But it was the best fight event they had seen in years, until the Red Sea incident with Moses."

Similar accounts of military defeats by divine intervention have survived. Two hundred years ago at the Battle of Waterloo, south of Brussels, the army of Napoleon Bonaparte fled from the combined forces of England and Germany. Again, accounts of angels and fire were whispered by the survivors.

Now, archaeology teams searching for World War I artifacts in the region have uncovered the telling evidence of the time – a 'Gneisenau' stealth jet with an 1815 French cannon ball lodged in its underbelly. Dr. Phaap says the find definitely places the aircraft in the Waterloo campaign and the cannon ball indicates the French showed deliberate aggression. Germans had developed jet engines long before the rise of Adolf Hitler and one or two of these aircraft would have been enough to scare off the entire French army of the time.

Medical Evidence on George A. Custer
The social problem of sloth is nothing new. But refusing care and attention in a time of war definitely elevates sloth to the status of carelessness. It can be hard to prove, unless documents can be produced that attest to criminal woolly mindedness.

After the death of Lt. Col. George A. Custer and many of his cavalrymen at the 1876 Battle of the Little Big Horn, his cause of death was reported as two gunshot wounds, one to the right chest and one to the head. Also, charges of recklessness and foolhardiness were attributed. However, further light on the nature of his alertness before the battle may be gleaned from retail records which did not come to light until 1937.

The Hop Sing Chinese Laundry Co. in Detroit, Mich., kept records on the famed soldier's uniforms and they disappeared in the 1870s. But detailed analysis of the records, once found, revealed that Custer undoubtedly had been given the wrong undergarments before his big fight. Instead of size large, they were size medium.

Dr. Phaap said the effect of constrictive undergarments would have had a dangerously crushing effect on the hero, affectionately dubbed 'hard ass' by his soldiers.

"It probably knocked him off his horse and killed him even before the first Sioux or Cheyenne realized who he was," he said.

Attempts to bring the laundry clerk to account for this dangerous omission so far have not succeeded.

38.   Why Cheering Sounds Silly

Have you ever sat in the bleachers at a football game and felt a tad uneasy? How about yelling when your kid scores a goal and feeling you have lost control of your wits? Rest easy, because you are in good company.

It doesn't take a professional sleuth to discover why. All you have to do is write down the words you are shouting and it becomes plain. It amounts to choral gibberish. It's done because no one else in the crowd knows anything else. It amounts to cultural and group illiteracy.

Take the standard cheer – *hurray*! This expletive is actually derived from an old sailors' exhaled chant when they were hauling cargo up by means of a rope. It relates to 'hoist' and could mean they are taking a merchant's luggage up from a ship's hold, or hanging someone by the neck. Variants of *hurray* are the hold-time *huzzah*, used during the American Revolution. It's older and much closer to *hoist*.

Just think for a moment. When you are celebrating something, like a new sales tax, or the arrival of Madonna's newest geriatric negligee, remember the word picture of grunting medieval stevedores with hernias and bad teeth.

Here are a few others, to give you pause before you utter one more specimen of this silly drivel.

BoooYa – You hear this cheer all the time when you're around the U.S. Marines. But I'll bet they never use it when they're advancing on the enemies of Freedom. It is derived from bouillabaisse, the classic French seafood soup, and it came from the Corp's tours of duty in the Mediterranean. To the unaware, it sounds like they don't know any other nouns.

Wooh Wooh Wooh – I think it was meant originally to resemble the deep, inexpressible feelings one experiences after belching, brought on by a sports result that is pleasing to the rest of ones fellow primates. *Hooray* is better.

Oskee Weewee – This is the official cheer of the Hamilton TigerCats team of the Canadian Football League. It runs *Oskee Weewee, Oskee Waawaa. Holy Mackinaw. Tigers Eat 'Em Raw*. If you yell and pronounce all this in unison with a crowd, it proves you are as inebriated as the rest of them and unlikely to freeze to death on Sunday game days.

Sieg Heil - To the minions of Nazi Germany in the 1930s and 1940s, this was the cry heard around the world – until the world woke up and silenced them for good. It means *Hail, Victory,* and normally you won't hear it repeated in anyone's company. Still, if you want to give it a try, it's your funeral.

Eleleu, Pro Libertate and Oohrah – On the other hand, these are the authentic battle cries of the ancient Greeks at Marathon, of Sir William Wallace at Stirling, and the U.S. marines in general, respectively. They were and are very effective at scaring the enemy, but should be left alone by everyone else.

The best cheer for anyone unconnected with anyone is: Kiss my royal Canadian ass!

Best Used when Running From Rottweilers – Mom!

When Walking Down the Hallway to be Fired – Bite me. And crappy New Year!

Walking Down the Aisle – No more curfews, no more sex/ In your dreams is coming next.

Answering a Yelling Child at Night – You called me and now, fool, you've got me!

39.   Your New List of Recycled Movies

No one is talking but computer graphics wizards have managed to capture famous film faces and images from DVDs and superimpose them on lesser films. The results are these grade B films that are for sale at half the price of the originals.

The Dork Knight – A would-be clothing salesman dresses in black to appear slim. Christian Bale's role is dubbed by the pre-recorded voice of Louis Armstrong.

The Radiator – In ancient Rome, a heroic inventor is abducted by subversives from the chariot trade and enslaved. Russell Crowe, as a luckless army veteran, produces radiators and transmissions before these too are smashed by a sinister wagon maker.

The Green Mule – Tom Hanks and his gang of merry prison guards lead a double life by entering community parades with a mule that is painted lime green.

Farmzilla – Godzilla, the giant walking reptile, escapes from his subterranean jail to discover that his city-smashing role has been downsized by Hollywood producers. He emerges as a benevolent tyrant who ploughs farm fields for free and digs irrigation complexes with his big toe.

The Latex Matrix – Grim in appearance and wearing long, black raincoats and sunglasses, a team of painting/construction gurus secretly coats buildings with latex camouflage, before looting all the appliances and fixtures inside. Keanu Reeves stars as the crowbar specialist.

Guts, Glory, Rum – The best vehicle of all for actor Sam Elliott, who uses chemicals internally to emote, before combing his eyebrows with a towel and riding his horse to some other place.

The Shawshank Exemption – In a slick scene transfer, an ensemble cast headed by Morgan Fairchild and Morgan Freeman overcome militaristic keepers and lead their people to a glorious, Promised Land. Watch for the cameo by Eleanor Roosevelt as a rebellious belly dancer.

The Godbrother – In a cozy, 1947 setting, banker Vito Corleone and his sidekick, Al Pacino, play practical jokes on neighborhood bullies with their machine guns. How they do it in blackface is an absolute miracle of cosmetics.

Pulp Diction – With the same throbbing, electric-guitar soundtrack, a nerdy group of high school grammarians infest Los Angeles with their annoying brand of criticism; lots of laughs from John Travolta as he dissects the Gettysburg Excesses.

Forrest Frump – In this animated tale, a group of well-meaning country creatures gang up to aid a well-meaning but unattractive housewife who happens to live in the woods. What's really special here is the tribe of gophers who sing as they remove burrs from her clothing.

Seven Samurai Sushi – The trials and tribulations of a Russian family who inherit a sushi franchise. The compelling musical score could have done without the polka music.

Once Upon a Time in the Chest – Henry Fonda, in a darkly tragic role as a cancer cell who invades the lungs of a smoker.

The Mound of Music – Earth is invaded by a huge pile of singing rocks, who only do Elvis impersonations. They are sent back into space by John Wayne and the Sons of the Pioneers.

Full Metal Galoshes – the U.S. Marines don raincoats and compete in a glee club festival.

The Lord of the Swings – Elijah Wood leads a gang of school yard toughs who fight off youthful feminists for control of government-funded playground equipment. Jackie Chan shines as Gollum, the bald kid on the slide.

40.   New Companion Animals

Ever since human beings figured out they were smart, they have kept pets on the family food dole. In exchange for the most revolting suppers, their fellow mammals have become their companions and have sucked up to them big time.

Normally, the mind turns to dogs when companion animals are considered, even though over time, such diverse species as anteaters, ferrets and canaries have filled out their ranks. Even wild animals like civets, mongoose, deer and spiders have been employed by human beings as friends. Not so with sharks, which rank in esteem well below tarantulas and praying mantis on the humans' trust scale.

But modern times have ushered in new directions for companion animals, especially since television media worldwide have devoted hours of air time on documentaries about seeing-eye dogs, St. Bernards (even though these are Catholic), and apparently psychic lemurs. Of course, the dogs get the most schlock and awe when it comes to admiration, but they have surprising limitations.

Seeing-eye dogs always rally a crowd when they go out in public. But, if they were allowed outdoors in places like Manila, in the Philippines, and Ho Chi Minh City, in Vietnam, most would never return to their masters. It's not so much a lack of care and respect on the part of an expensive golden retriever, but the sure knowledge they usually end up in a street vendor's cooking pot. The money loss is horrendous if you consider a golden retriever's average price tag - $1,000 – and that's before its training of two years.

As upsetting as it is to westerners, dogs are a food staple in many parts of Asia and Africa, with centuries of tradition – and recipes – to back them up.

Also, it must be remembered that now most people realize that animals never go to heaven, they should be put to better use here on Earth.

Sharp-eyed entrepreneurs are beginning to get the hang of new markets for companion animals, focussing on parts of the world where the niceties of cuteness and affection play lesser social roles. Here is a brief summary of the most notable ones.

Reptiles
Once you remove a crocodile's sensitive smelling organs and place patches over its eyes, it's just as sensible to danger as any poodle. These monsters actually adapt well to walking on a leash and also have been known to listen avidly to readings of Shakespeare and Chairman Mao, but the statistics of long-term employment are low because few owners have responded to our enquiries.

Vermin

These reviled residents of the sewer and garbage dump have survived for so many centuries because adaptation is one of their strongest talents. They remember their names and answer speedily when they are called, but they really are companions for the indoors. Another upside for these rats is the cheapness of their replacements – usually free. They respond well to obedience drugs like novocaine and crackers and will go meatless for days if budgets don't permit it.

Insects

Few people would allow that insects, like your average house fly or cockroach, possess or even deserve a personality. But the average consumer never realizes that some human beings cannot afford even to befriend a rat, with the prices of housing and chocolates these days. So the luxuries of personality and loyalty are passed by in favor of hearing a simple buzz, perhaps in the Arabian deserts where no one else lives, or the international space station, where nearly everyone else speaks Russian.

Bacteria

It is a true statement that bacteria represent the only culture some people will ever encounter. But these little beings actually are very helpful, when injected into the human or mammal bloodstream. Their presence will shorten the life of a man or woman suffering acute boredom and they will bring gaiety and giggling to mental patients who simply cannot cheer up.

Stuffed animals

After the laughter subsides, the wise observer will realize that many people can never tell the difference between a cocker spaniel and a teddy bear. They are simply too wrapped up in their jobs or marriages. It's one reason why these 'alternative animals' have been highly prized as gifts for centuries. In rare moments of lucid thought, a cost accountant may be disappointed by his Barbie doll's reticence, but these never end up in a pound, or a dump.

41.   Should You Renovate Your Home

Some years ago, Kansas farmer Elmer Worrall noticed a very strange thing. Cars were coming down his road, Lower Mountain Rd., slowing down in front of his house, and then speeding up. In a few minutes, they would return, slow down, then speed up and disappear. This went on for a few days and mostly, he forgot about it, because of his farming chores.

A few days after that, his wife came up to him while he was milking the cows, and told him, "Mr. Worrall, you had better come along with me!" She placed him in the pickup, backed it out of their gravel driveway, and headed for the main highway. Then she pulled over in front of a placard-type sign. It read: "House for Sale. 3613 Lower Mountain Rd." and an arrow pointed in what would have been their direction. Mr. Worrall felt sheepish, as a felon would if caught stealing horses.

A further investigation turned up two squirming boys, their sons, Travis and Elmer Jr. Both confessed to making and posting the sign. They said they felt they needed a new home because their own was too old and still had a two-hole outhouse in the back. Travis was caught because Mrs. Worrall knew he couldn't spell the word SAIL.

Mr. Worrall took matters in hand and had a one-toilet bathroom installed. But he didn't stop there. He painted the entire exterior of the home, even though it was soon to become an historic site, and he put in some vinyl, double-glazed sliding windows as well.

The whole moral of this story is: keep a better lookout on your boys. But the 'furthermore' is more important than the 'moral' – always hide your two-holer.

It's family secrets like this that get a whole renovation project dreamed up and off to the bank loan officer. In my case, a large woodpecker was at fault. We were hearing loud pounding outside our bedroom wall and on checking, we saw the bird banging away at our wood siding. He or she had found some grubs in our wall and wanted a full course meal. Even further checking, by a lady house painter, revealed we had two sparrow nests up under the roof overhang.

I responded by going to the hardware store, buying a steel slingshot, and firing big ball bearings at the woodpecker. For a while, I had to speak around the corner of the house, squatted down, and then take careful aim. But then the woodpecker started noticing me, like the fabled American snipers, and would fly off before I could pull a steel bearing from my mouth and insert it in the leather pouch of the slingshot. Once or twice I nearly gulped down the hearing, because the tension was terrible. And the neighbors would gather, cheering for the bird.

One thing led to another and we had the whole exterior renovated. It was so successful that we replaced our chain link fence out front and it stood out so much, our next door neighbor became furious. He hated our rancher-style fence so he put up a new one of his own, with solid wood panels. His place started looking like the Alamo, right next door to Lassie's farm.

With all that glorious history in mind, here are a few tips to help you decide what to do, if the health authorities find your personal two-holer, or if a woodpecker comes for lunch.

1. If you decide to renovate, always try to find and remove anything else that is embarrassing. In our case, a previous owner had split his cable service so that some tenants down in the basement could watch television and get emails. Another time, he mixed copper wiring with aluminum wiring behind his dryer, so no one would notice. The whole blame thing is, mixing wires is a short trip to the mortuary and cemetery – death by fire.

2. Try to find out if your spouse handles change well. If he or she doesn't, it qualifies the one with the short temper for a two-week stay with the relatives.

3. Always be security-aware. Hide your building materials under a tarpaulin and put rocks and topsoil on top of it. Would-be thieves will think it's for landscaping and shun it like

the measles. Also, if a man comes to the door offering to help with renos, always say no and call the police. He's trying it all over the country: it's his way of getting your food and cash.

4. Finally, when it's all done, have your picture taken outside in front. People will figure you for a genius, instead of the lazy loser they always thought.

PART THREE

42.   All About Crows

First things first: crows are not taking over the world. Far from it, they still would carry on as they are, even if our vaunted human race climbed one day into one giant airliner and left the planet.

Much has been made of crows. They are highly social birds with amazing abilities. They are the central images of several ancient religions. They recognize individual human beings and often follow them for miles. But not one crow has even so much as invented a cheeseburger; they simply eat what we leave over.

There is nothing sinister about their ancestry either. When dinosaurs roamed the earth, there were birds. Also, in the oceans, there were sharks; same as today. Every time a Tyrannosaurus Rex casually threw away another animal's drumsticks, a crow surely was there to snap them up. Given enough time and opportunity, any crow could consume a shark or dinosaur, as long as it lay still long enough.

Crows simply have not developed or even imitated mammals. Quite on their own, they have maintained a highly complex social society. To this day, they will gather on their own and have choral festivals, singing such anthems as 'The Battle Hymn of the KFC Roof' and 'Misty With the Decomposed Skin'.

Most crows live only 16 years maximum. One old bird lasted for 59 years, but it was fed in a cage every day, like many people in nursing homes and prisons.

Crows actually play organized games, sometimes with sticks and other objects as tools. They lead monogamous lives, usually staying with the same mate for life. The reason they gather in large flocks (called 'murders' of crows) is because they go trolling for dates among the singles groups.

The greatest enemy of crows is not mankind. It is the Great Horned Owl, that awakes each night just as the crows are heading for their nests and a night's sleep. This is when they are the most vulnerable and why crows hate Great Horned Owls. Furthermore, the owls usually decapitate crows before feasting on them.

Also, while generally avoided, crow meat is actually quite tasty, even gamy, and there are no prohibitions on killing them for food. This apparently is the reason that one unusual crow developed the ability to speak English to a family in upstate New York.

Identifying himself as Carlos, the male crow started speaking to one Larry Tremblay on a June night in Newfane, N.Y. He urged Mr. Tremblay to stop eating hamburgers and salads and begin eating Great Horned Owls.

"Great Hornies," Carlos claimed, "taste great when deep fried in small morsels and their eggs are very flavorful."

Indeed, Great Horned Owls weigh about four pounds and have wingspans of up to five feet. They are commonly found across the entire Americas and in addition to crows, they feed on and keep in check a huge vermin resource.

"We want peace with humans," Carlos said to Mr. Tremblay, "but if crows and humans are to have any future together, we must eliminate the hated owls."

Mr. Tremblay drew attention when he reported these and other conversations to the local law enforcement agencies. Few discernable results were observed.

His last time with Carlos was spent in discussing how peace in the Americas depended on mutual understanding and increased education for the unbelieving public.

"We come in peace," announced Carlos the owl. 'Next week, I go to Tunisia on the same sacred diplomatic mission."

(This interview was concluded abruptly when several senior ravens clustered around Carlos and took him away. He was muttering about 'the directive' but his statements grew indistinct.)

43.   Making your personal crisis work for you

Instead of cringing when bad things happen, you can improve the outcome by deciding how to react. When you yell the usual reactions, like 'Mommy!' you might as well admit to head lice.

What's worse: the National Enquirer gets tape of you running nude from a flaming motel; or you create a *Just Do It* placard to wave over your head?

Here are a few examples of useful advance strategies for those unexpected interludes:

The family that sold you as a child to the gypsies now discovers you are successful and rich.

1. Tell your foster parents where your real ones live.
2. Rewrite your will, leaving your debts to your real parents.
3. Don't die until your parents do.

A naughty person has sprayed you with pheromones, animal scents attracting unwanted attention from great danes.

1. Rehearse in your best, garlicky Bulgarian accent, "No spik Inglish!"
2. Don't go to the fragrance counter in your heavy tweeds.
3. Lie back and think of getting neutered.

The winter snows have melted and you notice the corpse of Vito Corleone, 'the Godfather', on your back lawn.

1. Save him as a lawn ornament for Halloween.
2. Leave him and let the tax man finish the job.
3. Never leave old pizza out overnight.

Due to a magic spell, Prince Charming thinks you are a big mac.

1. Avoid wearing sesame seeds on your buns.
2. Dress as a smoked sardine to scare him off.
3. Leave a trail of fresh French fries to Burger King.

Your family doctor discovers a nasal growth resembling John Travolta.

1. Wait until it grows into Mel Gibson.
2. Use it to explain your Bronx accent.
3. Use it as an excuse to stuff beans up your nose.

You are named 2010 poster boy for Planned Parenthood.

1. Change not only your name, but your Michael Jackson aliases as well.
2. Avoid mugging at family photo shoots.
3. Never wear mascara, even when out with your best girl.

You discover your worst enemy caught in a leg-hold trap.

1. Assess the resale value of the pelt.
2. Get a confession, in writing, to anything.
3. Watch your own step.

City work crews have discovered the baby teeth that your parents threw away.

1. Terminate your guilty fantasies about the tooth fairy.
2. Reduce, reuse, recycle, refuse. The baby teeth won't fit anyway.
3. Grind the old teeth and mold them into a soother, saving it for troubled times.

44. Some Gut Instincts You Should Never Ignore

We all have them – gut instincts – and they are there for a reason. So here are some of them and why you should never go back to watching TV until facing them.

1. You feel someone is watching you. Right now.
   Putting all your guilty feelings aside (like you are actually dancing nude in front of a photo of Bill Clinton), consider having a competent expert search your living room for concealed surveillance cameras. They don't make whirring sounds like in the old days, but one quick clue is clicking sounds whenever you leave the room. The camera mount might need some WD40.

2. You know something terrible is about to happen.
   Don't worry so much. Terrible things happen all the time. Just check your wallet and make sure your outhouse is still standing.

3. Your dog keeps staring you in the face and whining.
   First, check old Rover for little annoyances – a rubber band on his tail or a moving creature in his teeth. He might just feel sorry for you. If all clear, go to the doctor and have him check for catastrophic symptoms you've never noticed. Check the sky for approaching asteroids.

4. You notice a dinosaur going through your garbage pail.
   You have an absolute right to be afraid. Hide the family, open tins of sardines and throw them at the beast. It will attract bears that will drive the T-Rex away.

5. You just know something wonderful will happen today.
   Good for you. But keep checking all the small details, because maybe someone else wants you gone. That would be good for them.

6. A love letter arrives from your old high school flame. You hide it.
   Take action right now, because life is short and few chances remain. But if you are married, hide it at the bottom of a bird cage, where it will be safe for years.

7. At work, someone strange is sitting at your desk.
   He could be lost and eating his lunch, or yours. Maybe you are about to be laid off. And maybe, you are on the wrong floor.

8. During his sermon, the pastor keeps glaring at you. And you are only smiling at him. There's only one explanation other than approaching damnation. You forgot to wear your dentures today.

9. You are convinced your brother will soon visit you to borrow money. Check to see if it's pension day, or welfare Wednesday. Next, guess the worst time of day for a visit. Third, go to his place and ask for money.

10. While watching a movie, you notice that people are running away, screaming. Wake up. You are driving.

45. Night of the Hunter

The first rule of life in the jungle is this: never attack large animals. They smell bad to begin with and their breath is even worse. Instead, start on hamsters and work your way up.

Always attack when your prey is weakest – in mating season. They're always focussed on Miss Lemming or Miss Beagle and couldn't give a rip about you.

Never pounce out of trees unless you are using a short bungee cord. Never around your neck.

The best weapon to use is an air horn. Grab your prey first, fire off the air horn, and bounce back into the trees.

Be selective when purchasing hunting supplies. If the store clerk notices you around the whaling harpoons, he'll phone Greenpeace and they will freak out on your roof. And they won't come down until the media arrives.

Always decide first what you want to do with your catch – make barbecued raccoon perhaps, or whip up some squirrel salad. Never make egg salad from eagle or hawk nests unless you are sure the bird isn't home.

Mushrooms are good for salads, but always try them out first on someone.

Spiders are tricky. Never eat one without a firm grip on its beak.

Remember, even Davy Crockett started out as a small-timer. Before you tackle a bear, try wrestling with a big black poodle first.

If you want war paint for your face, always avoid yellow and spray it on with your eyes closed.

46. Heroes of the Animal Kingdom

Behind every great animal, there lurks a strong female.

1. King Kong. This hyperactive primate is famous for his movie roles – damaging huge skyscrapers while never harming a hair of the blonde chorus girl in the palm of his paw. But I bet you never heard of King Kong's sister, Ding Dong. When King was a kid, Ding made him sit through a dvd of *Peter Pan* at least once a day. So years later, he thinks he's friends with Tinker Bell, and Mr. Kong <u>believes</u>.

2. Elmo. You know the orange hairball from Sesame Street? He talks like a kid, screws up more than a cross-eyed barber and still gets love. His girlfriend, Lana the Land Shark, phones him before bed every night, tells him scary thoughts about the next day and hides his meds. So, Elmo is an undiagnosed sissy and gets paid for it.

3. Ariel the Mermaid. You know how sometimes she grows legs, goes ashore and lands a big male hunk of a human. Well her mother, Flora the Flounder, rubs her with Tiger Balm before each date. Turns out if Ariel has been ashore more than three hours, she smells like a dead catfish with athlete's foot.

4. Willy the Killer Whale. Everyone loves Willy and works in all his movies to free him from the nets and snares of naughty fishermen. He's loveable, but he got his start as a petty criminal, mugging innocent salmon and then, eating same. Years ago, Mona, his mom, weaned him off dairy products and got him addicted to seafood.

5. Barney the Dinosaur. He's a large reptile with a purple skin eerily reminiscent of iodine. Little kids play with him all day and return to their families in safety. This wouldn't have been so without Velma the Skunk, who taught Barney to play nice, back in Baptist Sunday School.

6. Benji the Terrier. Famous as one of the cutest little dogs to appear in film anywhere, he was unknown for much of his life because he couldn't bark without a lisp. However, Mother MacDonald, a saintly woman of Edinburgh, showed Benji he had no speech impediment at all. He had a Scottish brogue. After that, auditions and even a little pee break on the Red Carpet brought Benji the fame he deserved.

7. Jiminy Cricket. Once the lead food sourcer in a deadly plague of locusts, Jiminy converted to Mormonism after getting stuck on flypaper in Salt Lake City. After a year of indoctrination by Sister Julie Bumfitt, Jiminy re-entered society dressed like an Irish jockey and singing like a drugged-out Walt Disney. He is featured in "Pinocchio".

8. Squanto the Bulldog. Before getting himself famous, Squanto achieved notoriety by acing a 'B' on the senior chemistry exam at Notre Dame University, South Bend, Ind. His professor, Mary Agnes Smelt recognized his true talents and got him promoted to team mascot at all the big football games. In that way, he got all the glory and didn't make the chemists look stupid.

9. Harvey the Horse. Raised on an aristocratic estate in England, he carried his owner, Sir Ponsonby Colborne, all day in the 1815 Battle of Waterloo. (Sir Ponsonby actually was a notorious female novelist.) Harvey's owner tried to cheat death by hiding in a well, but just before the battle ended, Harvey yanked his rider out and got them both killed by nervous French sharpshooters. The dying horse was loudly applauded by the French, before they surrendered. They tossed the novelist back into the well.

10. Steve the Stork. The last in a distinguished line of medical informants who delivered all the babies to expectant parents, Steve lingered for a bowl of crabmeat offered to him by Lucretia Borgia, the noble poisoner of Florence, Italy. He never made his obstetrical delivery and the authorities turned that contract job over to physicians instead.

47. Your Alien Abduction Checklist (from my last time)

1. Always keep a backpack under your mattress. It contains: deodorant; toothpaste; reversible briefs, in case you stay more than a week; fire extinguisher (it worked on the Alien, the Borg, and Lex Luthor).
2. Check your granola each morning for crop circles.
3. If all your clocks start ringing at once, take a big breath and go to work. It's just Monday.
4. If a naked grey man with shaved head and big eyes examines you, never ask for dates.
5. If the aliens let you wander, find a big cannon and aim it at ISIS. Shoot. Over the alien loudspeaker, tell ISIS you are Mohammed.
6. Eat all the food they give you. Drink all their wine. Never ingest their Dristan.
7. If you meet Elvis, ask to meet Priscilla too.
8. If you have to share a bunk with an alien, always let him have the teddy bear.
9. Wear your dentures upside down. It freaks out their security guys.
10. Never trust an alien hooker, because of her boyfriend , the walking eyeball. You will see what I mean.

48.   Make Money by Starting Your Own Religion

One of the best job choices ever, right up there with pop diva, neurosurgeon and pharaoh of Egypt, for thousands of years has been: founder (or leader) of a popular religion. You are instantly recognized, financed and beloved.

Yet, few have ventured along this job path in recent years. The economy to be sure has devastated believer contributions of all kinds and the reduction of spirituality to mathematics lately has taken off much of the gloss. (x $plus$ $5 = God$). Who would want to be a martyr for that one?

Selecting the Best Beliefs

If you want to develop a great career, with extravagant finances, acceptance by your friends and lasting respectability, you are better off to select a belief that your converts would wish to espouse. Without doubt, the best method is to copy the organizational models of some successful religious groups and morph them with some new galvanizing force.

Even though the Catholics started on Rome's Vatican Hill, they could have selected the nearby and lesser known Pemmican Hill, a few miles to the south of the Vatican Hill and populated since forever by indigenous peoples from prehistoric Russia. Today, we call them the Indians and the Romans for centuries have called them the Huns. If they had worked that out, Catholics would be dressed in buckskins and feather bonnets, instead of the emperor's new clothes. It would have saved a lot of trouble in the winning of the West years later.

Building an Edifice
Every great religion erects a huge church. The examples make up a very long list: Istanbul's Hagia Sofia; Montreal's Oratory; Anaheim's Crystal Cathedral (now a Catholic cathedral with the demise and bankruptcy of the Hour of Power). That's got to be your number one priority. You might have to rent a school gym for a few months, but eventually nothing will galvanize your followers more than a splendid building program.

If you have fused spiritual beliefs with the wisdom of honey bees, for example, you might well consider getting a team of architects and developers to work up a subdivision of giant beehives, where the inhabitants are lulled to sleep nightly by enormous clouds of addictive smoke. The spiritual leader would have to be the queen. What better life than that for a bully?

Make the Music Work for You
We all have loved the Mormon Tabernacle Choir for decades. But not when they started off as the Mormon Triple Trio. When they experienced the makeover from warbling 1950s pop tunes to wailing enormous anthems, they had to get rid of their old acts, including minstrel show numbers in blackface. Times had changed.

For any new religion, the old rules apply. Start off your morning services with big, belly-buster hymns, encouraging believers to vote Clinton and Bill Cosby, or compelling them to declare war on Biloxi. Then, turn down the volume and moxie to gentler levels, just before you collect the offering.

Remember – all women prefer their male soloists to have a nasal, tenor voice. Drives 'em nuts. All men love to marry women with buck teeth. Think this through. You'll get more marriage fee income than a drive-through parson in Vegas.

Don't Be Afraid to Collect Your Accounts Receivables

The laborer is worthy of his hire. Doing religion is labor-intensive work and you should never be timid when passing around the collection plate. No one ever asks for their money back. It's the rules. Just continue buying your clothes, cars and other possessions at thrift stores.

Making Your Son the Heir-Apparent
It's only wise succession planning. Just like the other leaders in your new profession, always groom your son to succeed you. Sure, he's no entrepreneur and he's likely duller than you, but believers expect nothing less.

Create a good direct mail program
The members of your group will each want to have a physical object to remember you by. Nothing creates cash flow more than this. Advertise coffee mugs, neckties, glassware, cutlery, with your church name and get a good stamp machine. Then cruise thrift stores for your stock.

Torture vs. Shunning: exit options for Followers
Expect it when people quit. Just handle it right. Always send a card of sympathy, with the address of the nearest 12-Step program. The discipline is up to you.

Serving the Best Pancake Breakfasts Ever
If you want more camaraderie with lower cash outlay, serve up pancakes. Syrups are good, but in a harsh economy, spread the pancakes with strawberry jam.

Creating a Great TV Program
Use cable access and here's a neat trick: employ marionettes to spread your message. Remember the old Punch & Judy shows? A few correct strokes with a big stick on stage helps keep folks in line. And production costs will never trouble you.

...And if You're Worried this is Right for You
Do not go outside in any electrical storms. If you fail at this work, try selling insurance.

49.   Tri-Moxie Siddle's Tips for Getting Dates With Men

1. Go where the men are.
2. Give out money.
3. Take Notes.
4. Show up for the dates. Accept donations.
5. Take photos. Write a book.
6. Retain all the money, buy new clothes and repeat in another town.

50.   The Delirium Dictionary

Have you ever wondered about the English language? Do you know the last words of Zulu King Cetshwayo kaMpande before he was arrested by the British military? Why will we never know the name of the seventh wife of King Henry VIII?

The answers to these and many other delicious questions await the reader in a new release of The Delirium Dictionary, by the Sewanee Institute. Spokesman Dr. Amos Phaapp commented, "We always strive to know what the modern-day reader wants – what is uppermost in his or her inquiring mind – and we relegate past issues to the past."

Indeed, entries such as how reef knots may be measured in terms of gallons, and who actually stole the Israeli crown jewels, have been deleted from the dictionary. But they are still available in older editions, stretching back to the founding of the Sewanee Institute in 1854. It seems as though modern-day readers are no longer interested in the answers.

Dr. Phaapp said, "Questions about the English language are increasing as each month goes by. Recently, a veteran English teacher wrote us, asking now that English has become a universal language, if it could be left to locals in foreign countries to interpret word meanings and grammatical syntax – at will."

The Delirium Dictionary now allows such forays into experiments with grammar and spelling. For example, the word 'ballerina' was once burglarized and stolen from the Italian language and illegally inserted into English. Since then, the spelling of 'ballerina' has been unaffected by vowel endings – two ballerinas, hence, should have been spelled *ballerine*. But now, more modifications have been proposed. *Ballerina* would apply to a youngish female ballet dancer, but *balleroona* would apply to a ballerina past her prime.

We posed another popular question to Dr. Phaapp: "Why is this book entitled The Delirium Dictionary", since it sheds much light on difficult areas.

Dr. Phaapp's reply: "We don't care to share."

Moving on with the Zulu question, one of the more difficult questions of modern times, the new edition of the book claims, "Cetshwayo kaMpande, 1834-1884, the son of Mpande kaSenzangakhona, of the Zulu royal family, was arrested following his defeat at the Siege of Ulundi. Seeing he was betrayed by the son of a friend, he asked 'Was your father a friend of mine for so long that you should do this to me?" The chips which fall from this entry will dog scholars for decades. The king died under mysterious circumstances a few years later and the truth still remains a dark secret. In truth, everyone connected with the case is dead.

Reviewers of several past editions, notably the 1904 and 1949, have suggested the title's 'Delirium', was adopted by the Sewanee Institute in a back-handed response to accusations the compilers of the editions were demented.

Apparently, the identity of the seventh wife of Henry VIII, kept a state secret for centuries, was actor Mickey Rooney. Dr. Phaapp reported that this newsy piece of history was discovered by chance, from Mr. Rooney's rejected application for service in the U.S. military. His reported date of birth, Oct. 11, 1544, rendered him too old for any branch of the service, except for the Library of Congress. Further checking substantiated Mr. Rooney's birth certificate, which was counter-signed by both His Majesty and by Gen. George Washington. Both are now deceased.

A significant portion of the dictionary gives unprecedented focus to "Six Expert Lessons in the Art of Travel Photography". Close checking of the article's provenance reveals that Dr. Phaapp was the author and that most of the photo subjects are his wife, Honor Capone Phaapp. The eminent scholar has since been accused of using his wife's bikini photos to pad out blanks created through a shortage of scholarly reportage.

Dr. Phaapp's response: "Assuredly, the camera does not lie!"

Much can be gleaned from a cursory read of the dictionary's end notes, found near the end of each volume.

For example, it seems that Napoleon Bonaparte, learning of his definitive defeat at the 1815 Battle of Waterloo, exclaimed, "Well. That changes everything!"

Even the venerated Hubble Telescope, an epitome of aerospace research and development, was not invulnerable to criminal minds. What purports to be free tickets for rides on the telescope, can be found tucked in to the dust jacket.

51.   Flash Mobs and the City of the Future

As civilizations go, no real correlation may be drawn between popular music and a great nation's decline. Indeed, the glorious Roman Empire sank into the haze of history with its citizens, aristocrats and mobsters alike, singing "Funiculi, Funicula" in ribald enjoyment. The famed British Empire quietly dissolved while people in pubs sang "God Rest Ye Merry Burglar Men, Let No One Steal Your Swag".

Therefore, no great social upheaval can be discerned with the rise of flash mobs in urban centres. A fairly recent phenomenon, they were invented by political subversives who sought to disrupt public events; such as union organizers looking for new members in New York's St. Patrick's Day parade. Currently, they are little more than attempts by cheeseburger-hungry students hoping for approval and dates through You Tube.

(To be accurate, flash mobs involve the sudden appearance of performers, one after the other, among crowds of shoppers in public commercial spaces. Usually, they perform selections from popular classics like the Hallelujah chorus and 'Bohemian Rhapsody'. Finally, they shut up and dissolve back into the crowd. They originated in the U.S. Civil War, when bored platoons of northern soldiers suddenly sprouted from the cornfields of the old South and sang 'Blue Suede Shoes' to day shifts of indignant black agricultural workers, who preferred 'Old Black Joe'.)

What in fact looms for today's cities is a sly program designed to change the way modern people shop and do business.

The only thing preventing them from unleashing this commercial mayhem is the difficulty of organizing competent singers so that they perform together, using words that can be identified quickly by the average shopper. Most people cannot read sheet music, so they must be rehearsed time and time again, to sing together in cadence; the alternative is a white noise of muttering that sounds like old crows perched on a wire.

Once the singers can produce songs that are easy to follow, placing them in crowds is merely a matter of military drill.

The Initial Launch
To lull suspicious minds, your first two flash-mob outings should be innocent. Get hired by a chain department store to promote infant clothing sales and train the choir to deliver '*Lullaby and Good Night*'. The wives will march into the store while their unsuspecting husbands nap. Later, with cute little booties, the wives may announce the forthcoming pregnancy.

Later on, when the same crowd notices your singers quietly mingling next to them, and suspects more of the same mush, order them to belt out, 'Pay checks are higher when unions conspire', sung to '*My Favorite Things*'.

Restoring Public Order
Often, public gatherings get out of hand. This is a perfect opportunity to get hired by government or police authorities to dispel mobs quietly, quickly, cheaply and efficiently. All you have to do is rehearse the right words before the buses deliver your choristers to the scene of any riot. Once they mingle, have them softly sing, 'My Country T'is of Thee', and the rioters will immediately stop yelling and start hugging each other. In minutes, you will have the most hardened urban terrorists sobbing uncontrollably.

Then have the choir continue to these orderly song-directives:

(To *The Star-Spangled Banner*)
O say can you see
That the bozoes are here.

(To *I Had a Dream*)
I had a dream that I was thin,
Whatever dress size I was in.

Flakes on a Plane

Suppose an airline is having troubles with repeat air rage offenders and sharp lawyers have enabled these yahoos to board any plane they want. Once the airline hires you, all you have to do is assign two skilled flash mobbers to be seated on either side of this loser.

To begin with, the female mobber starts caressing the rager and working him/her over with smooches. The male mobber, who is crunching raw garlic with his teeth, starts pinching his target. In no time they will have the offender in handcuffs and begging for merciful treatment.

Targeting the Enemy
Most slum lords are active in their church communities. Twin mobbers work well also when seated alongside a slum lord or two, but larger groups interspersed with a congregation are far better at shaming during a church service.

Their song selection: 'Summertime, and the muggers are lazy,
Tenants suffer while the rats ask to dine.
Oh your mama's fat and your wallet is open,
So cough up, you bugger
Or your ass will be mine.'

Collecting Your Accounts Receivable
Say a man has died, owing you lots on his loan. Have four chanting mobbers show up at the funeral or the graveside and when all are gathered, start singing thus:

'Fill the grave with Uncle Charlie,
Fa la la la la, La la, la, la.
We're the bank that's got his Harley,
Fa la la la la, La la, la, la.'

Then just have the mobbers remove their hats and pass among the mourners with collection buckets.

52.　The Love Child of Batman

Years ago, when she was growing up, Eunice B. became suspicious, more and more each day, that her small town parents were different from all the others she knew. She wondered if she'd been adopted, because her parents never answered her questions. They never attended church or shopped at the mall.

To begin with, they never wore underwear. Even though she was polite enough never to watch them getting dressed in the morning, she did manage a few quiet looks when they did their laundry. All her father, Batman, washed was his large wardrobe of tights – black ones with muscles sewn into the front of the chest and leotards with tiny pockets arranged around the 32-inch waistbands, for holding Kleenex and breath mints.

As far as she could tell, her mother never wore clothes, as her ample layers of hair covered everything. Mama was the niece of King Kong and her given name, from the Asian island of her birth, was Ding Dong. She left Batman before Eunice entered kindergarten and her father became responsible for her care and upraising. Her personal attendant was Alfred Beagle, Batman's butler, and Eunice decided to take Alfred's surname.

"I never once had a Halloween costume," she was recorded as saying, during a government hearing on her entitlement to Batman's personal fortune. "I went door to door, trick-or-treating, in a cape Alfred made up of Mom's old hair clippings, and everyone thought I was a black cocker spaniel."

One day when she was seven, Eunice decided to watch her father, just for little things. Right away, she began to learn that he was different from other men. To begin with, he actually was not a man.

"The way I could tell he was coming home was the fruit flies," she said. "They would always be around when he was. All he really ate after all were pieces of fruit and the occasional flying insect. He really was a giant bat. All I remember of Mama eating anything was food she stole from the neighbors. Everyone thinks monkeys eat bananas, but they actually live on stolen stuff. There were days she would give me pop tarts and weekends I would get whole pies."

The experience of puberty was another challenge for Eunice. She recalled it in interviews as being "mostly natural" but she began to have troubles with hairy moles. Huge strands of hair began sprouting from points ranging from her ankles to her scalp and only the shaving efforts of Alfred the Butler saved her from the painful taunts of high school acquaintances.

In fact, when Eunice volunteered to join the U.S. Marines to fight in Vietnam, Alfred managed to get an unnoticed bunk near her barracks for basic training. She was Private Beagle now and when she was assigned to jungle warfare school near Saigon, Alfred could go no further. She had to fight the Viet Cong terrorists alone, and her hair literally exploded all over.
"One day as I was walking through the rice paddies," she later recalled, "I noticed large crowds of country peasants running away from me. Many were carrying AK 47 assault rifles and grenades, but still they ran away from me. My officers noticed this and right away, I was promoted to Marine Guerilla, first class. I hadn't shaved in four months and must have looked like a walking hairball."

After that, Eunice spent her active duty with the Marines, over four combat tours, as a walking fright. The Vietnamese, always first in personal hygiene - and shaving - were scared to death by tall people in bushy hair. All Eunice had to do was fire one or two shots in the air and yell, "Fur Ball" and chaos always followed.

Following the hostilities in 1974, Eunice was quietly demobilized and turned loose in the countryside near her childhood home. Reunited with Alfred Beagle, she recovered from the long trauma of war and retired to leisure in her old familiar Bat Cave.

"I accepted life as it came to me," she explained. "I watched a lot of tv, got laughs from the Rambo movies and grew really fat."

Acceptance died in 2013, when Alfred, on his deathbed, told Eunice a dark secret. She was not the natural daughter of Batman and Ding Dong, but her father's best friend, Katy Keene, another super hero. Keene, a 1950s-era high school model, had joined Al Qaeda in 1995 and had exploded herself in a girl's lavatory by mistake, next door to the twin towers of New York - wrong address.

Eunice, through the deathbed witness of Alfred and a competent New York attorney, was able as Batman's only heir, to obtain 45 percent of Keene's fortune from Marvel Comics, have her moles removed, and launch a new career as a bar-cruising cougar.

She is expected to be the leading Democratic candidate when Bill Cosby formally announces his presidential campaign soon.

Her first pieces of proposed legislation: laws forbidding the adoption of human beings by animals and the better treatment of hairy women.

53.   Lessons on Shaving

One thing that makes men distinct from chimpanzees is we don't bite lice from each other's backs in polite company. Another is: we shave alone; a third is that we never shave each other at the same time.

This solitary act is one of the few permitted men in a social context. It's a good thing, because if we were caught doing some of the personal misdemeanors we practice in private, we would be banished to reform school, at least.

For instance, many men sing or hum songs while applying the razor to their faces. They never let others know the lyrics and for that reason alone, choral groups never perform outside bathrooms. Another is: we grimace a lot when we shave, much like people ascending the steps to the gallows. It's done actually to shave flat and to the very nub, any loose whisker. But it's overdone and overrated. So first, keep a straight face.

Here is a brief list of rules for shaving.

1.   Leave relationships out of it. Before I grew my first whisker, I imagined what shaving was like, to the point of actually putting cocoa on my lower face in front of a mirror and using a ruler with a metal edge (the kind nuns use when rapping your fingers) to remove

it in decisive strokes. I was interrupted by my father, who left the bathroom without saying a word and I decided to forget it immediately, if only to erase all memory of his guffaws.

2. Get going right away. My worst class in high school, chemistry, became a memory of hell when a guy pointed to my adam's apple for a girl I sort of liked. She smirked at the sight of whiskers sprouting untidily from my neck. Then they giggled and whispered. Maybe, in later years and with maturity, she learned to shave too.

3. Always wash first. Using a face cloth, soak it in warm water from the sink, rub it with hand soap and rub that into your face. Then rinse the cloth and your face. Rub more suds onto your face and before you begin, remember that you never inhale when pressing a soaking wet face cloth against your moustache.

4. Never use long strokes with the razor. Always proceed gently and with short strokes, sometimes backing up a little to catch the odd hair. You can begin anywhere on your face that you like, and change any time. Most men begin at the left sideburn because they are right handed and don't have the imagination to begin under the nose and go counter clockwise.

5. Practice the laws of Zen. Believe it or not, you can close your eyes while shaving. Just be careful at certain points, like the right sideburn which can disappear quickly when you're daydreaming about Britney Spears. Or Hillary Clinton. The safest spots are the cheeks and front of the neck. (Leave the back of the neck to the barber, or else your level haircut at the nape of the neck will suffer and you will never know it.)

6. Another Zen thing: you can shave in the shower, once you have applied soap to the rest of your body. Always do that first, because often after you shave you will forget to fix up your underarms, and all the rest. The best thing about Zen is that you can close your eyes and make up weird Dickensian surnames while rubbing yourself.

7. If you feel a sting and think you have nicked yourself, open your eyes. Don't panic. If you see blood, that's another thing. It's usually no big thing, but if you've cut your tongue, remember to hold it inside next time. The best thing is to slap on some more suds and it usually stops.

8. If you see a guy on the beach and he's asleep, resist the urge to shave him. Some people get very touchy about that. If it's a woman and she's overtly hairy, do the polite thing and quietly leave a note on her car windshield.

9. No girl will ever ask you to shave her, so don't worry about that either. Count your blessings because girls' hair is more wiry than a guy's and likely to bend your razor blade into a 'U'.

10. Every young man should grow a beard. This is really just to let you get it out of your system. The real secret to having a good looking beard is to have a strong chin. Otherwise, forget it.

11. If you prefer an electric razor, just play with it as you would with toy cars and let the big boys shave with blades.

54.   Am I Really Dead?

Every day, our hearts beat 100,000 times, sending huge volumes of blood to every part of our bodies. That adds up to 35 million heartbeats a year for each one of us, or 2.5 billion beats in an average lifetime. So what's the difference if one heart drops a stitch? Or two? Or how about a heartbeat revving up like a mix master whenever one of us harbors a naughty thought?

With just those two ideas in mind (math here may not be spot on) Dr. Amos Phaap, of the Swanee Institute, was asked about the whole thing. Here's a transcript of the interview:

Q. Dr. Phaap, with all those hearts beating at once, who's to count everything and how come?

A. That's like having to answer the eternal question, "How many reef knots are there in a gallon?" I think what you really wish to know is whether you are dead or not.

Q. Thanks, doctor. That's probably a better one. But even if I'm dead at the moment, or perhaps the average citizen wishing to know, how can I tell?

A. It's tough, because while checking your pulse would be the obvious choice, if you were really dead, you couldn't, because when you are dead you cannot move your fingers one centimeter. It's like having your body frozen like novocaine. Perhaps if you could look around you, you could see some of your dead relatives hovering over you.

Q. That's a good one. I can see a few now, but all I see are three deadbeats and they're my wife's brothers. And they're all asleep in front of the tv.

A. Okay fine. You're probably alive, but hide your wallet and car keys under your butt.

Q. Okay Dr. Phaap, what's another way to know if I have, ahem, passed away?

A. Right. Let me suggest a visual suggestion. Two goats making love on a leather couch.

Q. Now stop a minute. I can see it, but it gives me heartburn.

A. Very well. Here's another image: Hillary Clinton on a slice of toast.

Q. White or whole wheat?

(ed.: the next few minutes of the transcript are garbled by expletives.)

Q. So, Doctor Phaap, I'm working out like crazy at the gym and the loudspeaker is pumping out "My Sharona" and all of a sudden, I see bursts of light and a ringing sound and everything goes blank. When I wake up, I am lying down on the gym floor and standing over me are all six Charlie's Angels, along with Wonder Woman. They're all spitting and saying 'blecch!' Now does that mean I've died and gone to heaven?

A. No. They're still alive. You just passed out. But before getting up, check to see if you remembered to wear your shorts.

Q. Thanks doctor. Are you a medical doctor or are you a psychologist?

A. Glad you asked. I studied at Night School Inc. in Denver and stayed so long, they offered me a doctorate, or an IFF degree. I took the doctorate.

Q. What was the IFF?

A. It stands for Incredibly Fine Fellow. Nice, eh? Any more questions, young man?

Q. Sure, doctor. How much do I pay you for this consult, or is it covered by welfare?

55.   Hi, Crazy Face!

Facial Recognition Technology, (FRT) a blast of questionable fragrance from the world of criminal justice, poses new challenges for every citizen. No matter where you go, your image shows up in the data banks of surveillance technology and the files of – who knows? It relies on the salient features of your face, the familiar triangle between your eyes and the bridge of your nose. If you are simply walking into a Starbucks one moment and participating in a riot in the next, someone in a short haircut and blue shirt will recognize you and maybe tell your mother.

However, be of good cheer. There are ways to defeat and foil this new monster and to turn the tables to your own advantage.

The easiest and cheapest way to frustrate the FRT police is a disguise. Remembering that FRT always searches for the eye-nose-eye triangle, you could start by growing longer bangs down your forehead; small wiglets also will do here.

Warts are a great option, even if you can't manage growing one on the triangle. Oliver Cromwell, a common man who ruled England in the mid-1600s, had a wart on the center of his chin, just below the lip. However, in several portraits, the wart can be seen in other parts of his face. Few realize that in his middle age, sly old Cromwell started a comb-over because he had grown bald. Assuming that pattern baldness is just like having a big wart on top of your head, you could consider investing in a fake bald skull cap. Moles and other marks of distinction can be glued to your face and re-pasted depending on where you might not want to be seen – in lineups outside a Chippendales performance perhaps, or in a roller rink on Fat Ladies Night.

Next comes aboriginal war paint. The stalwart First Nations warriors knew this and developed trademark brands in colors over the centuries to frighten off assorted incursions by unpainted Spanish, Chinese, Viking and English settlers. In your case, do a new face-paint with reflective pastels that would fool the most precise camera. If you are a man and a face-paint virgin, the best place to get help is the cosmetic counter at your best department store: the experts there could turn a two-week-old corpse into a living Spice Girl.

Currently, the most effective FRT repellant is LED lights fastened to your hat. No one sees them blink and you don't look any more dangerous on the street than a French poodle. However, on a surveillance tape playback, your face simply disappears in a cloud of pixels.

Other good spots to install LED lights would be around your auto licence plates; the girlfriend you meet in public places; the sleeping homeless people who love to relax outside your place of business; or the place where you buy your tax-free cigarettes.

Camouflage netting worked wonders in wartime and may be an option for you now. Thinking of aerial surveillance on a super highway, a LED-covered tarpaulin stretched over the roof of your car could make you invisible to the airborne traffic police.
Turning the tables on all of this, FRT spoilage may just be the thing for entrepreneurial young police detectives seeking to infiltrate the forbidding fortresses of rogue states, motorcycle clubhouses and Singles' Night at the nudist colony.

Remember the stealth aircraft used by the world's superpowers, in surprise attacks on unsuspecting terrorists and backward villains everywhere? With the new anti-FRT spray paints, not only could you snoop around their criminal hideouts unsuspected, you could let your airplane idle in their adjacent parking lots while you go inside for a coffee.

You could always learn from nature. Killer whales are black on their backs and white on their tummies, to hide from their next snack. By standing still, some insects can mimic twigs, to catch unsuspecting mosquitoes. You could wear black, rub yourself all over with Vaseline like a garden slug - and pose as a student at many universities.

In today's military, they teach you how to construct a 'hooch'. It's a mound-shaped hut covered with green plants and you could hide inside it for weeks. You could get videos of your local don taking off his pants, or someone else's

Unfortunate facial injuries can always be faked or downplayed. In the case of a truly ugly face, you could throw people off by walking with a limp. Even better, work to remember that people will always like it if you smile.

56.   Vladimir Putin and the Golden Fleece

Few of *Argo*'s 50 rowers realized who the muffled figure in the ship's prow was. Even as a younger man, Vladimir Putin was a mysterious figure, rumored to have been Soviet intelligence's famous blond assassin in the James Bond film *From Russia with Love*. Others thought he was a Calvin Klein underwear model, predestined for greatness.

But like all great men, he was prone to brood by night. Lesser folk get most of their romances in their dreams; men like Putin make them up as they sail along. (To brood, all you have to do is fold your arms, tuck your chin into your adam's apple, and grunt a little.)

Putin, as Rower 49, was one of several world-famous men who took part in a voyage of the pentecoter, *Argo*, a replica wooden rowing galley with one sail that was taken to find the Golden Fleece, in Greek myths. Few written accounts of a re-enactment voyage of the storied *Argo* survive, but in one account, a daily journal for 2003 kept by Rower 28, the Swedish adventurer Beppo Sverdlin, one can learn tantalizing facts about the leader of Russia.

July 1– Putin never sleeps below decks with the other rowers. He always complains that they suck their thumbs in their sleep and whimper like little puppies.

July 6 – All of us have to wear loin cloths, wrapped around us for modesty. Most of us wear either linen or cotton to look authentic, but some stand out. If you look close at the one worn by David Cameron, prime minister of England, you can read '…property of Sheraton Hotel Corp'. (It's a hotel sheet he never reported to the front desk!) Schwarzenegger wears a rabbit fur loin cloth from his days as Conan the Destroyer. To me it looks like a huge fur diaper. Jimmy Carter, former U.S. president, holds his loincloth up with suspenders. What's he afraid of anyway?

July 7 – We navigate our course by the stars, just like the old boys did when they sought the Golden Fleece. We left the harbor of Rome, turned left at the bottom of Italy and sailed right through the Dardanelles and Istanbul into the Black Sea. The fleece was at Colchis, at the easterly end of the Black Sea. One guy, Bill Gates, woke us all up one night claiming that his GPS had us in the middle of Missouri.

July 8 – No one has yet seen Putin take a pee. I think he carries a coke bottle in his shorts.

July 9 – A bank of low cloud has formed some miles off our stern and seems to be shadowing us. Several times, Putin and others have swum toward it and returned hours later, with no apparent effect on their health or stamina.

July 10 – Today, we stopped at a small port on the Turkish coast, not far from Colchis, site of the famed Golden Fleece. Putin went ashore and returned, claiming he found another fleece.

July 12 – That bank of low cloud sailed right past us in the *Argo*. It turned out to be a Russian light cruiser. I think Putin has been using their bathrooms, and buying hamburgers in their cafeteria.

July 15 – Today, we were inspected by the Turkish navy. The whole boarding party was female and one wore the uniform of a full admiral. They left with half of our rowers and we had to row home at half strength.

July 20 - Finally, the Russian cruiser, which Putin called the *Lodka*, gently pushed us from the stern all the way to Istanbul. All that time, Putin stood on the prow of the battleship, facing the *Argo*, with his fists on his hips. He got a great tan. From Istanbul we took a taxi back to Rome. Two of our crew were sold to the Bulgarian gypsies to pay our fare.

July 21 – Putin announced that his fleece had been stolen in Colchis and he was going to return to claim it. That was the last we saw of him. I had other things on my mind, like getting from the *Argo* to a hotel in my loincloth. I just followed Schwarzenegger and all the babes we attracted. The End.

57.   A Brief History of Yelling

Not many people like the notion of yelling: it calls many old demons to mind, as when mother clanged a Teflon pan on father's head in 1963, when he came home drunk and smelling of Wind Song; or when the teacher overheard my murmurings against him and gave me the strap. Yelling usually leads to blows and while rousing at times (e.g. *Remember the Alamo*, or *Kill the Ref*) it is better avoided in favor of peaceable humming.

Now the poor cousin of yelling and the creator of much ruin, especially in the workplace, is the ill-spoken word. Without much forethought or discipline, little mumbled statements to workmates (e.g. *She wouldn't see an opportunity if it snapped her left cup*, or *Merry Christmas you old loser*) will lead to shouts, slaps and slobbered apologies every time. Some statements, even the littlest of things, will set people off to yelling, making rude facial expressions and gnashing their teeth on many thumbs.

Most people think that yelling began when Alexander the Great jumped off his great brindle warhorse in front of some Iranian prisoners of war in 329 B.C. and they began giggling at him – because the great conqueror had forgotten to put his shorts on under his kilt that morning. Those little tee- hee's led to a screeching Alexander and one of the first recorded atrocities, and we all know how our great leaders love to copy their own heroes. Napoleon Bonaparte idolized Alexander and would never let his men wear underwear while in action. It cost him dearly in the biting snows of Russia and the flea-ridden meadows of Waterloo.

More recently, the downtrodden people of Greece voted to wear their undergarments, in direct defiance of their political leaders, who wished to avoid budget cuts and thumb their noses at the European Union, by forcing underwear tariffs and nationwide nudity. As a result, those poor

Greek descendants of Alexander have had to make their own shorts and t-shirts at home ever since. The cries of the people will never be found in the dictionary.

Little statements, like "*She would look better in blue hair and diapers*," got their start during those hateful days in Athens.

As a humble alternative, it is proposed that certain words be avoided, with tact, discipline and practice, in the workplace, where many terrible consequences do occur. In fact, the whole American Revolution that began in the 1770s, was caused not by an embargo against tea, but the forced hiring of idle British soldiers in the rope factories. Laid-off Boston employees could never shake their annoyance at redcoats getting their beer money and many years of war and unpleasantness followed. (The offending word? *Downsize.*)

Here is a list of workplace statements that should never be uttered, anywhere and anytime. Focus groups and corporate analysis reveal that these little words lead to yelling every time.

- *Tis the season*
  Lazy advertising copywriters issue this bland alternative to creative, useful ad writing every November to usher in Christmas commercials and the annual shudders of the customer and bill-payer.

- *Utilize*
  The one-syllable word *use* is much better employed here. Using *utilize* instantly transforms you into a snot in a suit.

- *Ninja*
  This word essentially is used to imply that the object in mind is an active, competent agent of change and success. Too bad, but it raises the spectre of a wheezing man or woman brandishing a sharp instrument who yells Asian verbs.

- *Paradigm shift*
  Every poor slob thinks this means a change in the workplace. In fact, it refers to an obscure philosophical definition. Say *paradigm shift* and your fellow employees will stop bringing their wallets to work.

- *Proactive*
  Uttered and declared by know-nothings who wish to be seen as successful innovators, it simply translates to the rest of us as *unnecessary workload.*

- *Outside the Box*
  This is a catch-all phrase that will be received as *Someone who cannot find a job anywhere else.*

- *Standard operating procedure*
  It literally means *the same mind-numbing diet we've eaten since probation.*

58. Household Hints for Life Today

The rise of modern technology has generally defeated any notion of homebrew solutions to the knotty household problems of old. We don't have to clean our chickens anymore before Sunday dinner, but just figure out how to gather the bones with one hand afterward. Any burn holes in the carpet or couch can be solved by donating the whole article to the poor and replacing it at Costco.

But just hold on. We don't hear about whole families jumping up and down in gratitude for their first-class leg shaves or Barack Obama action figures. In fact, statistics prove that people in general are just as depressed as they ever were and resentful about their lot in life. They are a pouting, slouching lot and it's time for another look.

- What, for example, does one do about rough teeth? After all those dollars spent on dentists, the teeth still feel like corduroy when you run the tongue across them. Any orthodontist will tell you the teeth smooth out over the years and to just keep on licking. But we have better things to do. So, how about it? (The best remedy is a trip to the taxidermist, who stuffs all our hunting trophies. Ask him for a tin of bees wax, insert the contents into your mouth and lick on. Or, you can boil your dentures a little while. Try scrimshaw or having them filed to a stiletto point. You can look like a great white shark if you want to.)

- For cracked leather on your car upholstery, simply slice a cucumber into thin rounds and hook them together into a limp doily. That helps bring back that old tannery scent.

- Rub a fresh banana into your dingy underwear and wear it around the house for two hours. Your chubby thighs won't chafe now, no matter how your walking rubs them together, and your underwear will come out of the wash with an intriguing scent.

- Wasps invading your bird house? Install a vacuum cleaner underneath the bird residence and while the wasps are sleeping, simply suck them into the oblivion of your Hoover bag.

- Your dryer always turns itself off after 17 minutes? First determine who turned it on. Then, ask them for a longer setting the next time.

- You have been invited for adoption into a strange family? Check them out. First, ask if they are okay and then ask, why you. Are their communal peanut roasts a little too intricate? Or, are there fruit flies in their ice box.

- Request a sabbatical from your nephew. Pay his way to a nice Army recruiting station and give him books about how to build a sniper's hide. For your part, take a trip to a casino that offers long-term room rentals. Work off the room rents in the counting room. If the nephew ever returns, he'll never find you in prison.

- If you have finally learned to levitate, why not take the time to mentor a student? Prime candidates for instruction include Olympic wrestlers, janitors who have to change ceiling light bulbs and restless persons in a boring church.

- Tired of paying nearly $10 each week for new razor blades? Simply rinse the one you have after each shave and then spray with Tilex. It's guaranteed to stay sharp for at least two years, but remember never to allow a woman to shave her legs with it. Before she's done with one leg, her tough leg bristles will bend the splines, pry the lubricating strip from the razor head and pop its retaining strips, thereby compromising its torque for life.

59.   Body Language: Understanding the Messages

Our bodies speak to us most of the time, but are we paying attention? Are we like so many drivers who take their vehicles out for a spin and ignore the feedback signals sent from the dashboards? Yes, we are so preoccupied with the traffic and the road ahead that important information is ignored and forgotten.

When the mind is in pain, the body cries out. For so many of us, our minds are numb, conditioned by the noise surrounding us, and we disregard the signals the body offers. For example, a pretty woman walks in front of us and sweat breaks out on the forehead. To a body language expert, that means only one thing: there is an anxiety our fly is down. To the person with the sweaty brow, only a soft whistle will present itself. People need to get back in touch with what our bodies are crying out to their minds.

To assist you in re-establishing contact with your mind, here is a sample list of actual case reports, presented in a question-and-answer format.

Q. *Lately, while taking my morning shower, I've noticed that acupuncture needles have begun detaching themselves from my skin and falling onto the floor. What's up?*

A. Foreign objects like that mean only one thing. They're not falling off your body. More likely, your wife is trying to stop the smoking she's hidden from you all these years and is seeing an acupuncturist. In addition to her naughty habit, she is too lazy to pick up the needles.

Q. *Every time I watch Dancing with the Stars, I start coughing and can't stop. Is there hope I can last the season without barfing too?*

A. Not to worry. You'll make it to the final round. It goes back to when you were a kid and you used to hold yourself absent mindedly, because it gave you pleasure. Now, coughing has replaced that because the doctor told you to cough whenever he held you. So when that program is on, stop holding yourself.

Q. *An ugly growth has begun to develop inside my right nostril. It is grey in colour and looks like Mel Gibson. Any suggestions?*

A. You seem to have contracted an Australian wart. You can have a surgeon remove it, or wait for a year or two. It might come to resemble a wallaby. If you notice it is moving around, you might have a marsupial birth in your future. Check your medical insurance brochure for more info.

Q. *All my friends tell me I have bad breath. I've tried everything – tooth brushing, mouthwash, breath mints. What can I do?*

A. Your bad breath came more probably from your stomach and it could be a sign of limited nutrient breakdown. In addition to chewing your food more, you might try eating only yogurt and fruit. But if the smell is really from your sinus cavities, you need to have a doctor flush you out with Drano3. Your stomach might be backing up into your head. Or vice versa – have you checked your flatulence levels lately?

Q. *My kids tell me that a big map is slowly coming into focus in the area of my back, between my shoulder blades. What's up with that?*

A. It depends on what land mass the map shows. If it's a part of the globe, it's just a trick from National Geographic, to renew your subscription early. But if it shows the location of your nearest McDonalds, your body wants you to buy and eat more French fries.

Q. *My next-door neighbor's daughter is a dream kid. She's so nice in a world filled with rotten kids. When she sits outdoors, all the birds come and perch on her and the squirrels sit in her lap. Is she a saint or something?*

A. It's a sign all right, but not of any religion. The birds are there for lunch, for either head lice or fleas. The squirrels are always attracted to nuts.

60.   Famous Hauntings

More and more, entrepreneurs are fed up with dressing their wives in gorilla costumes and having them run through the local underbrush. The resulting videos definitely show a North American primate on a woodsy daytrip, but there isn't enough drama to cause a real scare and, ultimately, a steady cash income from tourists and science fiction propagandists out to see Bigfoot.

Ghosts are in order here and the requirements are trickier. You need to produce a definite chill up the spine and those guttural moments of terror before realizing one cent from your supernatural business plan. This goes way beyond computer graphics and the definite fright they would inflict on your banker.

As in all frauds, the real thing works here. You have to enlist the help of a real ghost, an actual spirit who once lived in an historical time. Unless they are here on a field trip, the famous spectres of Tudor England are not likely to cooperate, so you have to work on more recent tragedies like unhappy child stars from Hollywood or investment bankers overtaken in wealth by software prodigies in sweaters and beards. Both types are great sources of shrieks and moans.

Here is a list of ghosts who are likely to take you up seriously for a novel tourism deal.

Ho Chi Minh
The great architect of Vietnam's unification, he spent decades in the jungles in conflict with the Japanese, the French, the Americans and CBS News. Few know of his humble beginnings as Ignatz Fimmel, in Duluth. His greatest ghostly act is riding a tricycle through retail stores' shopping aisles and scattering cluster bombs. They don't hurt anyone when they explode, but so far, they've made many a shoplifter go straight.

Charlie Chaplin
He was always regarded over the years as one of our greatest comedians. And yet, was he really that funny? Sometimes watching his films, one wonders if he was overplayed by the studio promotions office. To think that he made his fortune playing homeless characters, one wonders if his whole act was a cry for help. For a small amount of cash, he will help promote television news footage by dressing as a C.difficile virus and showing up at vitamin stores.

General Isaac Brock
A true hero in the War of 1812, he was one of the most misunderstood. He got his start as a reedy youth whose waistline grew to 47 inches from eating rich Iroquois food in Canada. His girth alone frightened the Americans who thought he might have a heart attack at any moment. For extra cash, he will show up with Dolly Madison and crash golfing carts into police cruisers.

President Abraham Lincoln
Famous for freeing the slaves, he is less well known as a frustrated retail employee in a general store. Like most slaves, he too was stuck in a dead-end occupation. Only marriage got him out of it. He shows up as himself at bargain sales and tosses merchandise with Wild Bill Hickock.

William Randolph Hearst
This famous newspaper tycoon once instructed one of his war artists, "You furnish me the pictures and I'll furnish the war." He loves to frighten innocent terrorists and is the main reason they never show up for Valentine's Day parades in Syria.

Susan B. Anthony
The famous suffragette was endeared to history as one of the reasons women got the vote. But there were a lot of voting mishaps she is probably not proud of. Indeed, after all the recent scandals, she swore off voting and politics and now only appears at vegan parties, as Betty Crocker.

Genghis Khan
He never let a survivor escape and yet he is criticized in all the histories for being a mass slayer. Anxious to put that bum rap to sleep, he would consent to be a great draw for all those tourists from China. In a recent appearance he claimed he's been a bunk mate for decades with Emperor Nero of Rome: "All he ever does is suck his thumb and kick off his bedsheets."

Your Mother
She always was your biggest fan. She'll haunt you anywhere, but make sure she agrees to keep out of your bathroom. Even better is that nastiest mother of all time, Klara Belzmeer. She is famous for showing up at family weddings, when new spouses enter the realities of wedded blitz. All she does is go chin to chin with the new bride or groom, and wheeze, "Fresh Fish. Fresh fish!"

###

41707646R00057

Made in the USA
Charleston, SC
05 May 2015